fashion t•shirts

fashion t·shirts

easy sew projects for fun fashions

Lorine Mason

Creative Publishing
international

Author Lorine Mason has been a passionate sewer and crafter most of her life. As an active designer in the creative services industry, she works on a wide variety of projects during a particular year. Her designs can be found in books, magazines, on the Internet, and in pattern catalogs. She enjoys working with a variety of art mediums and keeps an open mind—which often results in one-of-a-kind designs. Lorine lives in Herndon, Virginia, with her husband, Bill, and two daughters, Jocelyn and Kimbrely.

Dedication

I dedicate *Fashion T-shirts* to my mom and dad. My parents, Henry and Mildred Schlamp have been married for 55 years and raised six children. Through their love and dedication to family, they have encouraged each of us to develop our talents and take great pride in our varied list of accomplishments. Thanks Mom and Dad for that love and encouragement over the years. Your loving daughter, Lorine

Creative Publishing
international

Copyright 2007
Creative Publishing international
18705 Lake Drive East
Chanhassen, Minnesota 55317
1-800-328-3895
www.creativepub.com
All rights reserved

President/CEO: Ken Fund
Executive Managing Editor: Barbara Harold
Development Editor: Sharon Boerbon Hanson
Photo Stylist: Joanne Wawra
Creative Director: Tim Himsel
Photo Art Director: Mary Rohl
Photographers: John Haglof and Steve Galvin
Production Manager: Linda Halls
Cover and Book Design: Mary Rohl
Page Design: Kiersa Notz

Printed in China
10 9 8 7 6 5 4 3 2 1

Library of Congress Cataloging-in-Publication Data

Mason, Lorine.
Fashion t-shirts : easy-sew projects for fun fashion / Lorine Mason.
      p. cm.
ISBN-13: 978-1-58923-298-3 (soft cover)
ISBN-10: 1-58923-298-4 (soft cover)
1. Fancy work. 2. T-shirts. I. Title.

TT750.M325 2007
746.4--dc22   2006024650

Contents

Using the T-shirt as a Canvas

Everyone wears T-shirts. In fact, a T-shirt is the perfect garment. While the basic shirt is unisex, it can reflect everyone's personal style. A T-shirt can be worn alone, under other clothing, layered, knotted, tied, rolled, or torn.

Painting, stamping, or sewing gives a T-shirt one-of-a-kind flair. The designs in *Fashion T-shirts* start with the basic T-shirt as a canvas, then transform them into wearable art with clever cutting techniques, stitching, stenciling, stamping, crocheting, or embellishing.

Follow the easy-to-read instructions and how-to photos, or let the designs inspire you to create your own one-of-a-kind garment, using a favorite technique and embellishments. My inspiration came from colors and patterns generated by nature and human hands. Find your inspiration and let the artist within you create your own special version of a T-shirt.

Before You Get Started

Read through this section to get off to a great start! Also read through **Cutting T-shirts and Measuring Trim,** and **Tools.**

The Ongoing History of the T-shirt

Over the years, the T-shirt evolved from an undergarment to the popular version we wear today. The T-shirt came to the USA during World War I after American troops, who sweltered in their woolen uniforms, noticed European soldiers wore light cotton undershirts. The Americans quickly adopted the comfortable garment.

Its shape led to its name and by the 1920s "T-shirt" became an official word in the American English language with its inclusion in Merriam-Webster's Dictionary.

During World War II the T-shirt became standard-issue in both the American Army and Navy, and although formally underwear, soldiers often wore them without an overshirt. After the war, civilians copied the soldiers. Soon T-shirts appeared with advertising printed on them.

The popularity of the printed T-shirt rose slowly, as many Americans still considered it underwear. The Silver Screen changed all that. Hollywood movie stars such as Marlon Brando, James Dean, and John Wayne offered the world T-shirt sex appeal. They wore their underwear in public and made it cool in movies such as *Rebel Without a Cause* and *A Streetcar Named Desire.*

Custom printed T-shirts eventually became popular souvenirs picked up at rock concerts or sporting events. Today, T-shirt designs signify patriotism, display attitudes and feelings, and show product loyalty and political beliefs. The custom T-shirt is now a portable billboard used by schools, retailers, sports teams, and corporations. The acceptance and popularity of T-shirts as casual wear continue to grow, owing to loyalty to sports teams, colleges, and universities, and recording stars, and to corporate logo T-shirt giveaways.

A recent study conducted by a leading T-shirt manufacturer found that the two top reasons for owning and wearing a T-shirt are comfort and the memories that a favorite shirt provides.

Now you can create your own custom designs and fashions with personal style and fun touches that satisfy comfort and provide a special memory for the wearer.

Helpful Tips for Sizing

It would be so much simpler if the garment industry used standard sizing for T-shirts. Since this is not the case, variations in cutting and measuring may be necessary. The basic T-shirt can vary in overall length and/or width from one manufacturer to another. Do not become overly concerned about fit. The designs featured in this book are not tailored designs calling for exact measurements and multiple fittings; they are about the creative process and the finished product.

In creating the designs featured in *Fashion T-shirts* some basic measurements will help you achieve the desired fit. In most cases you need only simple bust and/or waistline measurements. Purchase a T-shirt that fits comfortably around the bustline. If the finished design will be worn as a jacket, purchase a shirt one size larger. Remember to check the fabric content and allow for shrinkage when washing the shirt. Check the label, as some shirts are sold preshrunk eliminating the need to prewash. If possible, try on the T-shirt during the construction stage. If this is not possible, ask the intended wearer for her measurements.

A few designs require measurements be taken. "Midnight Seas" features a waistline tie. To achieve a good fit, have the wearer try the T-shirt on once the neckline is sewn. Mark the T-shirt at the wearer's natural waistline. Remove the T-shirt and lay it on a flat surface, measure 1" (2.5 cm) down from the initial marks, and mark the circumference of the T-shirt. The bias tape should be sewn using these markings to allow for the proper draping of this particular design.

The designs "Shades of Teal," and "Domino Duet" feature elastic casings across the back. Have the wearer try on the T-shirt, fit the front, and then gently stretch a piece of elastic across her back beginning and ending underneath the arms.

"Spring Zinnia" has elastic around the entire top. To determine the length of elastic necessary to provide a good fit, wrap a measuring tape around the wearer slightly above the bustline. Add 1" (2.5 cm) to this measurement and cut a piece of elastic to the total length.

You may want to adjust the length of the finished designs by removing less or more fabric from the hemline. The important things to remember are to have fun and to think creatively.

Cutting T-shirts and Measuring Trim

Every project except "Scarlet Flower" carries specific marking and cutting directions. Instructions often say to cut *only through the front or the back*. Read and follow the instructions carefully to be sure you don't ruin your project by cutting through too many layers.

When a project uses ribbons, lace, or another trim as an integral construction element (for example: the ribbon straps in "Domino Duet"), the length needed will depend on the size of the T-shirt being altered and the measurements of the person who will wear it. Be generous when measuring; it's better to have a bit too much rather than not enough as you sew.

Tools

The instructions for all designs in *Fashion T-Shirts* assume you have basic sewing tools and equipment when you begin a project.

Necessary supplies for each design are a fabric marker, a ruler, and all-purpose thread to match the fabrics.

A rotary cutter and mat are the easiest cutting tools to use, but you may choose to use a scissors.

Taking Care Before and After

Should you wash the T-shirt before starting work on your design? The choice really is yours. I usually do not wash a T-shirt prior to working with it. I do, however, purchase a high-quality T-shirt that is well constructed. I have also used secondhand T-shirts that have been washed many times. If you have concerns about shrinkage or colors running, take the time to prewash; then press the T-shirt before beginning your design.

Keep in mind the intended purpose of the finished garment and the type of enhancements used in the T-shirt design. In most cases the shirt remains machine washable; however, a few designs may justify hand washing in cold water. Read labels when purchasing trims, buttons, and other accessories. A delicate button or trim may move a T-shirt into the hand-wash category. The general rule is that the most delicate item in your design (unless removable) dictates the care required to maintain your garment. You have unlimited options, but recognizing the influence of the trims and the accessories on washing or wearing will keep your design looking great.

Basic Techniques

This section helps make your altered T-shirt project a success. Also read through **Cutting T-shirts** and **Measuring Trim**, on page 9, and Tools, on page 10, to get off to a great start!

Sewing

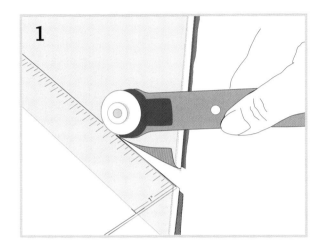

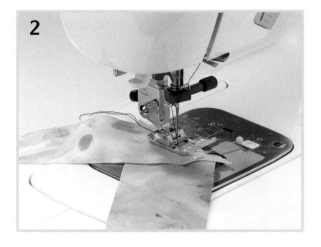

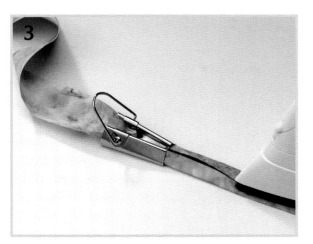

Bias Binding

1   Fold the fabric so the selvage aligns with the crosswise cut. Measure out 1" (2.5 cm) from the bias fold and cut the first strip using a ruler, rotary cutter, and mat. Cut all remaining strips 2" (5.1 cm) wide.

2   Pin the strips right sides together at a right angle and slightly offset. Stitch together using a ¼" (6 mm) seam. Press the seam open. Continue sewing the strips together to make one continuous strip of binding. Trim the points of the seams even with the edges.

3   Insert one end of the strip through the bias tape maker, following the manufacturer's instructions; pull the fabric strip gently through the opposite end. Press the folds in place as you work, taking care not to distort the width of the strip.

4   Form double-folded bias tape by folding the bias tape in half lengthwise, right sides out, and pressing.

Prairie-Point Trim

1 Cut 2" (5.1 cm) squares of fabric. Fold each square in half diagonally, wrong sides together, and press. Fold again diagonally and press.

2 Place one triangle under the sewing machine needle, with the fold to the back of the machine.

3 Tuck the folded edge of a second triangle halfway into the first triangle and stitch across the raw edges, adding new triangles as you stitch to create the length needed.

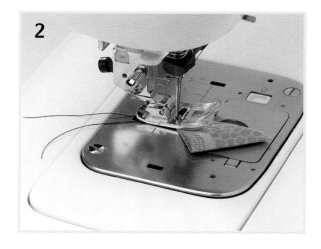

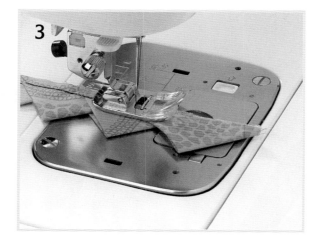

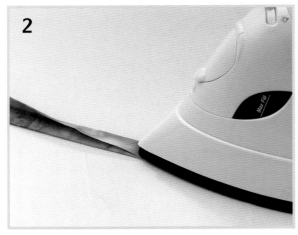

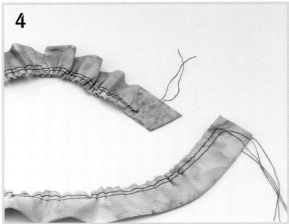

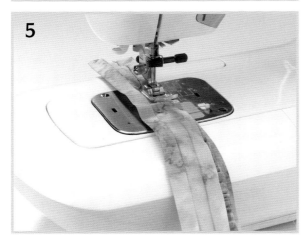

Double-Sided Bias Ruffle

1   Follow steps 1 and 2 under *Bias Binding* (page 12) to create a bias binding strip.

2   Fold the bias strip in half lengthwise, right side out and press.

3   Sew two rows of gathering stitches, ⅛" (3 mm) and ¼" (6 mm) from the raw edges, starting and ending ½" (1.3 cm) from the end.

4   Create two sections of bias binding the length required plus 1" (2.5 cm). Create a length of bias ruffle twice that length, following steps 1-3 above. Turn all bias binding and bias ruffle ends under ½" (1.3 cm) and press.

5   Sandwich the ruffle between the two bias binding sections, right sides together. Pin one end. Pull the gathering threads and distribute the gathers evenly between the bias binding, pinning through all layers. Stitch a ½" (1.3 cm) seam through all the layers.

6   Press both sides of the binding away from the ruffle.

Embroidery

Blanket Stitch

1   Work the blanket stitch from left to right. The first stitch of the blanket stitch differs from subsequent stitches. Insert the needle into the inside of the neckline fold (or in a side seam if the top fold is sewn closed) and bring it out in the crease. This will hide the knotted end.

2   With the needle held vertically, point up, insert it in the right side of the fabric, ¼" (6 mm) below the neckline. Bring the needle up from the back of the fabric, and tuck the thread under the needle. Gently pull the thread to snug the stitch to the neckline edge, carefully aligning the loop of thread along the folded edge of the fabric. Take subsequent stitches ¼" (6 mm) apart.

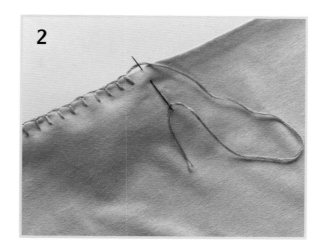

Chain Stitch

1   Bring the threaded needle up at the beginning of the pattern line and hold the thread down with your thumb. Insert the needle where it last emerged and bring the point up approximately ⅛" (3 mm) away. Pull the thread through, forming a loop, and keeping the working thread under the needle point. Repeat until the pattern is completed.

Running Stitch

1   Bring the needle and thread up through the fabric and then back down into the fabric in an in-and-out motion. The stitches should be approximately ⅛" (3 mm) long.

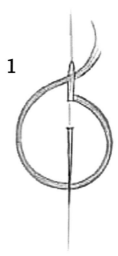

 Note: When working on a cut edge, insert the needle through the front ¼" (6 mm) from the neckline; then insert it through the back next to the cut edge to loop the thread.

Crocheting

Slipknot

1 To begin to crochet, you need to make a slip knot. Start at about 6" (15 cm) from the yarn end, and make a loop.

2 Insert the hook and catch the working yarn, drawing it up through the loop. Pull both ends to tighten the knot and then slide it up to the hook.

Chain Stitch

1 Start with a slipknot on the hook.

2 Yarn over and slip the yarn through to form a new loop without tightening the previous loop. Repeat this to form the length of the chain desired. End by cutting the yarn and threading it through the last loop.

Single Crochet

1   Make a foundation chain.

2   Skip two chains and insert the hook under the top loop of the third chain. Wrap the yarn over the hook and draw it through the chain loop only. There are two loops on the hook. Yarn over, and draw the yarn through both loops. Single crochet made. Continue working single crochet into the next, and all following chains, to the end of the row. To make the next and following rows of single crochet, turn the work and chain one. This is the turning chain and counts as the first single crochet in the new row. Skip the first stitch at the base of the turned chain and work one single crochet into the top two loops of the second stitch in the previous row. Work one stitch into the next and each stitch to the end, including the top of the turn chain.

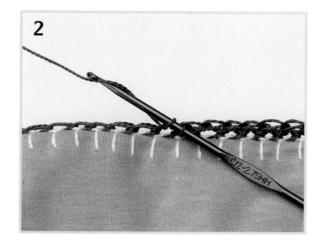

Double Crochet

1   Chain three.

2   Yarn over; insert the hook into the fourth chain from the hook. *Yarn over, draw yarn through the stitch, yarn over, draw yarn through two loops on the hook. Yarn over; draw through two loops on the hook (one double crochet). Yarn over, insert the hook into the next stitch, repeat from*.

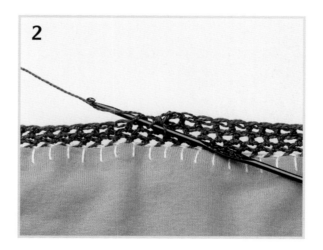

Triple Crochet

1   Chain four.

2   Yarn over twice; insert the hook into the fifth chain from the hook. **Yarn over, draw the yarn through the stitch, yarn over, draw the yarn through two loops on the hook, yarn over, draw the yarn through two loops on the hook, yarn over, draw the yarn through two loops on the hook (one triple crochet). Yarn over twice, insert the hook into the next stitch, repeat from**.

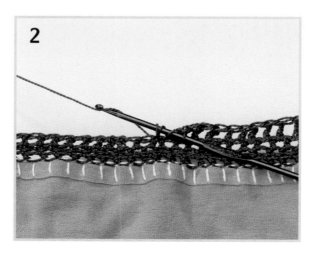

Beading

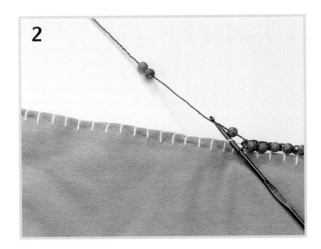

With Crochet

Project: Calypso Crochet

1. With a slipknot on the hook, insert it into the first blanket stitch, yarn over, and slip the yarn back through the stitch only. Slide a bead up to the crochet hook, wrapping the yarn over again, and slip the yarn through both loops on the hook. The first single crochet is complete. Insert the hook into the second stitch and repeat.

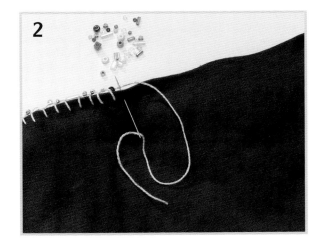

With Blanket Stitching

Project: Mulberry Beaded

1. Refer to step 1 under *Blanket Stitch* on page 15 to begin.

2. Insert the embroidery needle vertically into the right side of the fabric ¼" (6 mm) below the neckline. Bring the needle up from the back of the fabric, tuck the thread under the needle, and then slide a bead onto the needle. Pull on the thread to snug up the stitch, carefully aligning the loop of thread along the raw edge of the fabric. Take subsequent stitches ¼" (6 mm) apart and add a bead to every stitch.

 Note: Before beginning to crochet, slide the required number of beads onto yarn. Beads can then be slid into position as needed.

On Neckline Trim

Project: Fiesta Orange

1   With the right side of the T-shirt facing up, pull the needle and thread through to the right side of the fabric, slide a bead onto the needle, and take a stitch back into the fabric close to the edge of the bead. Come back through to the front of the fabric, and stitch in reverse through the bead before attaching the next bead.

Random

Project: Lime Sorbet

1   Pick up a bead and stitch into the garment using an embroidery needle and embroidery thread.

2   Bring the needle back up through the fabric close to the original stitch. Tie an overhand knot using both ends of the thread and trim the thread ends.

Hot-Fix

Projects: Black & White, Caribbean Ribbons, and Mulberry Beaded

Follow the manufacturer's instructions to adhere beads to the T-shirt.

Stamping & Stenciling

Hints for Success

1 Practice stamping or stenciling on a scrap of paper before beginning to work on a T-shirt.

2 Avoid overloading the brush with paint.

3 When combining colors, use a separate brush for each paint. Dab paint onto the stamp or stencil overlapping the colors to combine them.

Stamping

Projects: Calypso Crochet, Tricolor Tropical

If the stamped image is not sharp, clean the stamp with soap and water, dry completely, and begin again. Add fresh paint each time you stamp to achieve a uniform look.

1 Slide a piece of cardboard between the layers of the T-shirt. Tape the T-shirt and the cardboard to a flat surface.

2 Mix the acrylic paint and the fabric painting medium together on a plate, using a sponge brush and following the fabric medium manufacturer's instructions.

3 Dip the brush tip into the paint and carefully dab onto the surface of the stamp. Avoid getting the paint into the crevices of the stamp. Use a separate brush for every color.

4 Place the stamp on the fabric and press. Do not rock the stamp. Repeat as needed.

Stenciling

Projects: Spring Zinnias, Shades of Teal, and Coral Floral

You will be repositioning the stencil to complete the "Shades of Teal" pattern over the entire front. Allow the paint to dry before shifting the stencil. Tape-striping is used on "Shades of Teal" only. When using a stencil repeatedly, clean the stencil periodically to keep the image sharp. Wash the stencil gently with soap and water after use, and allow it to dry completely.

1   Slide a piece of cardboard between the layers of the T-shirt. Tape the T-shirt and the cardboard to a flat surface.

2   On the left side of the T-shirt, place six strips of 1" (2.5 cm) masking tape ⅜" (1 cm) apart on an angle, with the ends wrapped around the T-shirt hem. Add one piece of masking tape at an angle on the right side, ending on or at the top strip of tape on the left. Firmly adhere the tape to the fabric.

3   Set the stencil on top of the T-shirt and tape in place with masking tape.

4   Mix the acrylic paint and the fabric painting medium together on a plate, using a sponge brush and following the fabric medium manufacturer's instructions.

5   Dip the brush tip into the paint and dab onto the T-shirt, beginning at the outer edges of the stencil and working toward the center. Take care to avoid paint seepage between the stencil and the T-shirt. Allow the paint to dry before repositioning the stencil.

6   Dab the paint between the lines of masking tape. Allow the paint to dry before removing the tape.

7   Remove the tape from the left side of the T-shirt. Extend the strip of tape applied on the right side down to, and around, the hemline; add five more strips ⅜" (1 cm) apart. Paint, dry, and remove the tape as instructed in step 6.

Strappy Tanks, Camis, and Halter Tops

Perfect for the summer or a trip to the tropics. These designs are easy to make, easy to wear, and easy to personalize.

Calypso Crochet

Bohemian brown combines with techno-vibe dots to dance against an exotic blue background. One part hippie, one part techno fun.

materials list:

T-shirt, blue

fusible web tape, 1/4" (6 mm) wide

cardboard

paper plate

sponge brush

acrylic paint, burnt umber

fabric painting medium

rubber stamp

scrap paper

embroidery needle

embroidery floss, turquoise

three skeins DMC 5 pearl cotton, brown

six turquoise and three brown beads, 6mm

crochet hooks, US 2/C (2.75 mm) and US 4/E (3.5 mm)

two buttons, 1/2" (1.3 cm), turquoise

fabric glue

T-shirt Preparation

1   Fold the T-shirt in half, matching the shoulders and the side seams. Mark a point 3" (7.6 cm) down from the bottom of the neckline ribbing. Lay a ruler parallel to the bottom hemline along the 3" (7.6 cm) mark; measure 5" (12.7 cm) in from the center fold and mark. Also mark just below the armhole seam line. Draw lines connecting the three marks. Cut *through all the layers* of the T-shirt along the drawn lines.

3" (7.6 cm)

5" (12.7 cm)

Construction Details

1   Press the fusible web tape to the wrong side along both armhole edges. Remove the paper backing from the tape; turn under ¼" (6 mm), and press.

2   Press the fusible web tape to the wrong side along both edges of the neckline. Remove the paper backing from the tape, turn under ¼" (6 mm), and press.

3   Stamp the front of the T-shirt, following the stamping instructions under *Stamping and Stenciling* on page 20 and using the project photo as a guide.

4   Blanket stitch (page 15), along the neckline and armhole edges through all layers of fabric, spacing the stitches ¼" (6 mm) apart using the embroidery thread and needle.

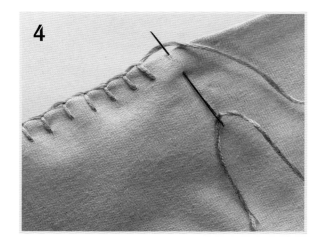

5   Thread the beads onto pearl cotton in the following order: two turquoise beads, one brown bead, two turquoise beads, one brown bead, one turquoise bead, one brown bead, one turquoise bead. Slide the beads down the thread until ready to use in the design. Refer to *Single Crochet* and *Beading with Crochet* on pages 17 and 18 respectively. Single crochet using the smaller crochet hook into the blanket stitch around the neckline and armhole edges, starting and ending at the left front edge. This ends row 1.

6   Continue crocheting following the instructions below for the front and back panels.

7   Starting at the left front edge, continue crocheting following the pattern on page 27 for the front neck extension.

8   Attach thread to the left back edge and crochet the back panel the same as the front, omitting the beads. Do not tie off the thread.

 Note: Beads are only used on the front panel. Omit the beading when crocheting the back panel.

Crochet Instructions

Rows 2 and 3: Single crochet in each stitch across.

Row 4: Triple crochet in each stitch across.

Row 5: Double crochet in each stitch across. Pin-mark the placement of 5 beads in the next row, centering them in the row and spacing them about five stitches apart.

Row 6: Double crochet in each stitch across. Pull up a bead up into each marked stitch.

Row 7: Single crochet in each stitch across.

Row 8: Double crochet in each stitch across. Pull up a bead into each stitch that is directly above the three center beads two rows below.

Row 9: Single crochet in each stitch across.

Row 10: Double crochet in each stitch across. Pull up the last bead in the center stitch.

Rows 11 and 12: Single crochet in each stitch across.

Tie off thread and weave ends into crocheting.

9 Chain four using the large crochet hook. Then triple crochet into the next four stitches. Turn. Repeat until the strap is 7" (18 cm) long. Tie off the thread. Tie the thread on at the opposite corner, and crochet another strap. Weave in the ends.

10 Sew a button to the front crochet panel at each corner. The buttons will slide between the crochet stitches, creating adjustable straps. Tie off thread and weave the ends into the crocheting.

t·tip

Change the look with exotic beads and threads. Eyelash yarns and hand made beads— what a combination!

Fiesta Orange

Beaded natural stone accents complement warm earth tones to complete this halter-top conversion.

T-shirt, burnt orange

fusible web tape,
1/4" (6 mm) wide

fifteen stone beads, 8 mm

embroidery thread

embroidery needle

T-shirt Preparation

1 Fold the T-shirt in half, matching the shoulders and the side seams. Mark a point 5" (12.7 cm) down from the bottom of the neckline ribbing. Lay a ruler parallel to the bottom hemline along the 5" (12.7 cm) mark. Mark a point 5" (12.7 cm) in from the center fold. Mark another point 3" (7.6 cm) down from the bottom of the armhole along the T-shirt side. Draw lines connecting the three marks. Cut *through all layers* of the T-shirt along the drawn lines.

2 Cut two strips for the straps 1½" (3.8 cm) wide across the width of the T-shirt, beginning and ending at the armhole seams. Trim away the sleeves along the armhole seam.

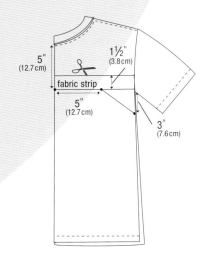

5"
(12.7 cm)

1½"
(3.8 cm)

fabric strip

5"
(12.7 cm)

3"
(7.6 cm)

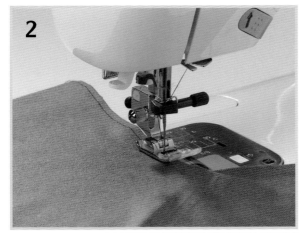

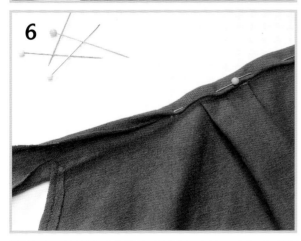

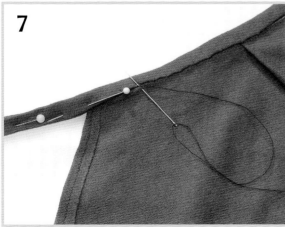

Construction Details

1   Press the fusible web tape to the wrong side of the T-shirt along the armhole edges. Remove the paper backing from the fusible web tape, turn under ¼" (6 mm), and press.

2   Topstitch close to the folded edge along the armholes edges.

3   With the front of the T-shirt facing up, place a pin at the neckline to mark the center point. Place an additional pin ¾" (2 cm) to the right of the center pin. Place a third pin ½" (1.3 cm) from the second pin. Fold the third pin toward the second pin, forming a tuck. Repeat the pinning and folding on the left side. Form three additional tucks on each side, gauging the distance between the tucks by fit. Stitch across the top of the tucks to secure.

4   With the back of the T-shirt facing up, mark the center point of the top edge. Place a pin 1½" (3.8 cm) to the right of the center pin. Repeat on the left side. Fold the outside pins toward the center pin, forming an inverted pleat. Stitch across the top of the pleat to secure. Remove all the pins.

5   Fold one of the 1½" (3.8 cm) strips in half lengthwise and mark the center with a pin. Lay the strip on the T-shirt center front, right sides together and matching the centerpoint pins. Stitch the strip to the T-shirt using a ¼" (6 mm) seam.

6   Press the strip up from the T-shirt edge. Fold the raw edge to the center fold of the strip.

7   Fold the binding strip to the inside of the neckline, and pin in place. Hand-stitch along the inside seam line.

8   Fold the raw edges of the strips toward the inside, then topstitch through all layers, creating straps.

9   Repeat steps 5 to 7 with the second strip along the back of the T-shirt.

10 Stitch the beads to the front of the T-shirt along the neckline, using the embroidery needle and thread, and following the instructions under *On Neckline Trim* on page 19.

Designer Extra, T-shirt Necklace

This multi-strand necklace with three rows of T-shirt tubing and decorative wooden beads accents a sassy look perfectly. Supplies include silver-tone metal chains, metal bead cones, a closure ring and clasp, split rings, and wooden beads. Use a pattern of overhand knots and beads to create your own personalized T-shirt necklace by joining together stands in various colors.

1   Cut three 1½" (3.8 cm) strips across the width of the T-shirt. Pull the ends of a strip taut, forming a rolled tube.

2   To insert the fabric tube through the beads, stitch through one end of the fabric tube using a needle and thread, then wrap the thread tightly around the end of the tube. Use the needle to thread the fabric tube through the bead.

3   Pull the beads into the desired pattern then tie an overhand knot before and after each bead.

4   Glue the fabric tube ends inside of the metal bead cones. Attach a section of chain to both cones. Repeat steps 1 to 4 with the other strips.

5   Connect one end of all three chains to a split ring, and connect it to the closure ring. Connect the other ends to a split ring, and connect that to the clasp.

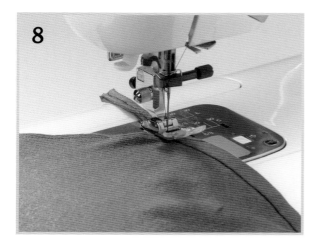

t·tip

Check out your local thrift stores for jewelry leftovers. Great prices!

Shades of Teal

A Bohemian inspired revival in teal! Complete the look by pairing this charming camisole with a shirred skirt or loose-fitting cropped pant.

materials list:

T-shirt, teal

masking tape

stencil

paper plate

acrylic paint, deep teal

fabric painting medium

sponge brush

fusible web tape, $1/4$" (6 mm) wide

elastic, $5/8$" (1.6 cm) wide

T-shirt Preparation

1 Fold the T-shirt in half, matching the shoulders and the side seams. Mark a point 3" (7.6 cm) down from the bottom of the neckline ribbing. Lay a ruler parallel to the bottom hemline along the 3" (7.6 cm) mark. Mark a point 5" (12.7 cm) in from the center fold. Mark another point 2" (5.1 cm) from the bottom of the armhole along the T-shirt side. Draw lines connecting the three marks. Cut *through all layers* of the T-shirt along the drawn lines.

2 Cut a strip 3" (7.6 cm) wide from the bottom of each sleeve. Trim away the seams, leaving two flat strips. These will be used in step 6.

3 Unfold the T-shirt and lay it on a flat surface with the back facing up. Place a ruler parallel to the bottom hemline, aligning the two side markings. Move the ruler up 1" (2.5 cm) and draw a line. Cut along this line *only through the back* of the T-shirt.

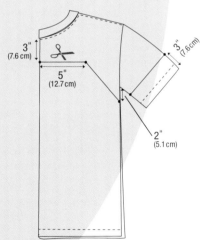

3"
(7.6 cm)

5"
(12.7 cm)

3"
(7.6 cm)

2"
(5.1 cm)

Back View

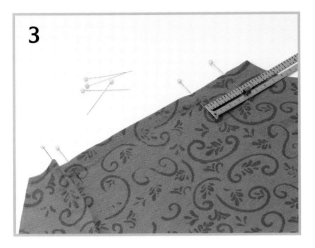

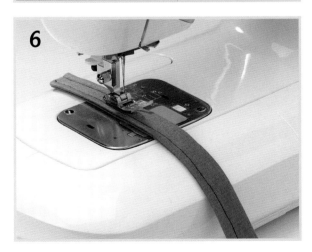

Construction Details

1 Stencil the front of the T-shirt, following the instructions under *Stamping and Stenciling* on page 20.

2 Press the fusible web tape to the wrong side of the T-shirt along the armhole edges and the front and back neckline. Remove the paper backing from the fusible web tape, turn under ¼" (6 mm), and press. Fold the back edge under 1" (2.5 cm) and press.

3 Place a pin 1" (2.5 cm) in from each side along the top front edge. Place a second pin 1½" (3.8 cm) from the first pin. Fold the first pin over to meet the second pin, forming a tuck. Pin the tuck in place. Repeat with the opposite side.

4 Topstitch around the circumference of the T-shirt, ¼" (6 mm) from the top edge. Topstitch along the back of the T-shirt, ¾" (2 cm) from the top edge. Remove all the pins.

5 To determine the length of elastic necessary to provide a good fit, refer to the instructions under *Helpful Tips for Sizing* on page 9. Cut a length of elastic. Insert the elastic through the casing in the back of the T-shirt, pinning the elastic at each end. Stitch through all the layers to secure the elastic ends.

6 Lay the strips cut from the bottom of the sleeves wrong side up. Press fusible tape along the cut edge of each strip. Remove the paper backing from the tape and fold inward to butt up against the sleeve hemline. Press. Fold the strip in half lengthwise. Trim one end of each strip at an angle. Topstitch through all layers of the fabric, ½" (1.3 cm) from each edge.

7 Stitch the straps under the front edge of the T-shirt.

Designer Extra - Thrift Store Makeover

Check this out—a $2 thrift store T-shirt made over into summer fashion fun. Consider the possibilities for your old team or school T-shirts. No one will believe you made it!

fashion t-shirts

Spring Zinnia

Spring into style with a breezy stylized halter-top resplendent with a graphic zinnia motif, rickrack, and button trim.

materials list:

T-shirt, lavender

zinnia stencil

masking tape

paper plate

fabric painting medium

acrylic paint, white and lavender

sponge brush

fusible web tape, 1/4" (6 mm) wide

rickrack, medium width

fabric glue (optional)

elastic, 1/4" (6 mm)

two buttons

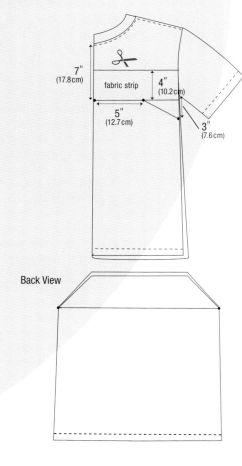

Back View

T-shirt Preparation

1   Fold the T-shirt in half, matching the shoulders and the side seams. Mark a point on the fold 7" (17.8 cm) down from the bottom of the neckline ribbing. Lay a ruler parallel to the bottom hemline at the 7" (17.8 cm) mark, and mark a point 5" (12.7 cm) in from the center fold. Mark a point 3" (7.6 cm) down from the bottom of the armhole along the T-shirt side. Draw a line connecting the marks. Cut *through all layers* of the T-shirt along the drawn lines.

2   Trim away the sleeves along the armhole seam from the upper cut-away section. Cut two strips, 4" (10.2 cm) wide, across the width of the remaining upper section. These will be used for making straps.

3   With the T-shirt back side facing up, lay a ruler parallel to the bottom hemline between the two marks at the sides, and draw a line. Cut along this line *only through the back* of the T-shirt.

Construction Details

1 Stencil the front of the T-shirt, following the instructions under *Stamping and Stenciling* on page 20.

2 Press the fusible web tape to the wrong side of the T-shirt along the top edge. Remove the paper backing from the tape, turn under ¼" (6 mm), and press.

3 Center the rickrack under the upper edge of the shirt. Stitch close to the upper edge, securing the rickrack. Overlap the ends of the rickrack. Seal the ends with fabric glue.

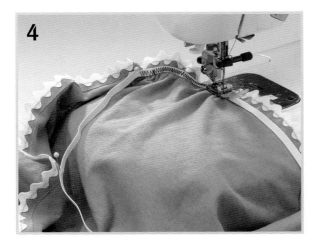

4 To determine the length of elastic necessary to provide a good fit, refer to the instructions under *Helpful Tips for Sizing* on page 9. Cut, then fold the required length of elastic in half and mark the center with a pin. Secure the center of the elastic at the inside center of the T-shirt back just under the rickrack trim. Bring the ends of the elastic to the front, and pin both ends to the inside center front. Estimate the amount of stretch needed when sewing by gently stretching, then pinning, the elastic at the underarms. Stitch down the center of the elastic, using a zigzag stitch and stretching the elastic as you sew.

5 To create the T-shirt straps, fold a strip in half lengthwise, right sides together, and stitch a ¼" (6 mm) seam. Press the seam open and center it. Stitch a point at one end, pivoting at the seam. Trim. Repeat for the other strap. Turn the straps right side out and press. Topstitch ¼" (6 mm) from all edges.

6 Locate the center front of the T-shirt and mark with a pin along the top edge. Mark points ½" (1.3 cm) from the center pin on both sides. Pin the straps with the inside edges at the pin marks. Attach the straps by topstitching through all the layers.

 Note: Half of the zinnia is stenciled with white paint and the other half with lavender paint.

7   Fit the T-shirt to the wearer to determine the placement of a buttonhole on the left strap. Sew the buttonhole according to the sewing machine manufacturer's instructions.

8   Sew a button on the right strap to correspond to the buttonhole. Sew another button at the center front of the T-shirt.

t·tip

Stencils come in a wide variety of styles and sizes. Do not limit yourself to traditional designs. The zinnia stencil used in this design was found in the home décor aisle of a craft store.

Domino Duet

What's better than one T-shirt design? Two!
The ribbon ties and buckle accents on this
fun duo are sure to turn heads.

two T-shirts, black

fusible web tape,
¼" (6 mm) wide

single-fold bias tape

elastic, ¼" (6 mm) wide

2 yd (1.5 m) ribbon,
⅞" (2.2 cm) wide

four plastic belt buckles,
1" (2.5 cm)

fabric glue

T-shirt Preparation, Camisole

1 Spread the T-shirt open with the front facing
up. Lay a ruler across the T-shirt parallel
to the bottom hemline and just below the
armholes. Place a mark under each armhole.
Mark the center front of the T-shirt
1½" (3.8 cm) above the armhole marks.
Draw a gently curving line from the center
mark down toward the armhole mark at
the right side. To match the left front curve
to the right, cut along the drawn line on
the front of the T-shirt from the right arm
mark to the center front, fold the trimmed
section to the opposite side, and use it as
a cutting pattern cutting *only through the
front* of the T-shirt.

2 Turn the T-shirt over and draw a straight line
connecting the two armhole marks along the
back of the T-shirt. Cut along this line,
cutting *only through the back* of the T-shirt.

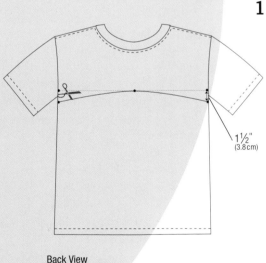

1½"
(3.8cm)

Back View

1½"
(3.8cm)

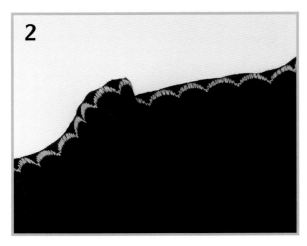

Construction Details, Camisole

1 Press the fusible web tape to the wrong side of the T-shirt along the top edge. Remove the paper backing from the tape, turn under ¼" (6 mm), and press.

2 Stitch along the top edge of the shirt using a decorative shell stitch on your sewing machine.

3 Pin the bias tape just underneath the stitched trim, starting on the front, 3" (7.6 cm) in from the side edge, then continuing around the back of the T-shirt and extending onto the front 3" (7.6 cm) past the opposite side edge. Fold the raw edges under and stitch along the top and bottom edges of the bias tape to form a casing.

4 To determine the length of elastic necessary to provide a good fit, refer to the instructions under *Helpful Tips for Sizing* on page 9. Cut a length of elastic. Insert the elastic through the casing, pinning it in place at each end. Stitch through all layers to secure the ends of the elastic.

5 Mark the desired placement of the ribbon straps on the front and back of the camisole.

6 To create the buckle loops, cut two 3" (7.6 cm) sections of ribbon. Slide one ribbon, right side out, onto the bottom of a buckle, then fold in half creating a loop. Stitch the bottom edge of the loop to the front of the T-shirt. Repeat with the other ribbon and buckle.

7 Determine the length of ribbon required to come from the back of the camisole, feed through the front buckle, then wrap around the wearer's neck and tie (This forms the front V-shape). Cut two sections of ribbon this length. Stitch the ends of the ribbon ties to the back of the camisole, right sides up.

t·tip

Even the most basic sewing machine models feature decorative stitches. Combine your favorite with one of the many varieties of thread available and you'll have a winning combination.

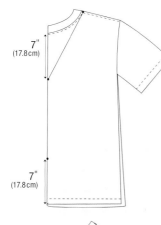

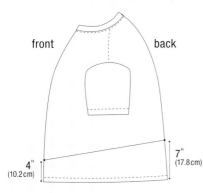

front   back

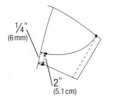

T-shirt Preparation, Shrug

1 Fold the shirt in half, matching the shoulder seams, and press a line down the center front of the T-shirt. Cut the front of the shirt open along the pressed line.

2 Mark a point 7" (17.8 cm) from the bottom of the neckline ribbing along the center opening. Draw a gentle curve from the mark toward the neckline ribbing at the shoulder seam. Cut along this line continuing around the neckline to remove the ribbing. Stop at the opposite shoulder seam. Fold the trimmed T-shirt section to the opposite side and use as a pattern to finish cutting.

3 Fold the T-shirt in half at the back, wrong sides together, and match the front openings. Mark a point 7" (17.8 cm) up from the bottom hemline along the center back fold. Mark another point 4" (10.2 cm) up from the bottom hemline along the center front opening. Draw a line connecting the front and the center back markings. Cut along this line *through both layers* of the T-shirt.

4 Measure ¼" (6 mm) along the sleeve seam line and mark. Measure 2" (5.1 cm) up from the first mark, and place another mark. Connect the two marks with a line. Mark the top of the sleeve at the hemline stitching. Draw a curve from the top mark toward the 2" (5.1 cm) mark. Cut *through both layers* of the sleeve along the drawn lines.

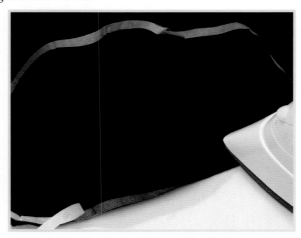

Construction Details, shrug

1 Press the fusible web tape to the wrong side of the T-shirt along the neckline. Remove the paper backing from the tape, turn under ¼" (6 mm), and press. Repeat at the front edge and then the bottom hem, and finally around both of the sleeves.

2 Stitch along the neckline, front, and bottom edges of the T-shirt, and around the sleeve edges using a decorative shell stitch on your sewing machine.

3 Mark the placement of the ribbon loops on the front of the T-shirt. Cut two 7" (17.8 cm) pieces of ribbon. Slide the buckle onto the ribbon and form the ribbon into a loop. Stitch the ends of the ribbon loops to the front of the T-shirt at the shoulder seams. To secure the buckle placement, add a drop of glue to the edge of the buckle and pinch the bottom of the ribbon loop closed.

Shrugs, Boleros, Cropped, and Babydoll Jackets

These clever cover-ups range from sophisticated to funky. Change the tone of the designs by altering the colors of the T-shirt and trims.

fashion t-shirts

Black & White

T-shirt, black

grosgrain ribbon,
1" (2.5 cm)

snaps

hand-sewing needle

1 yd (0.92 m) gingham ribbon,
⅝" (1.6 cm)

Hot-Fix Swarovski® White Pearls,
3 mm

Hot-Fix applicator wand

The dramatic contrast of black and white can be classic, sassy, or just plain fun—whether transforming a sundress into evening wear or topping a pair of capri pants and a camisole.

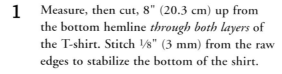

T-shirt Preparation

1   Measure, then cut, 8" (20.3 cm) up from the bottom hemline *through both layers* of the T-shirt. Stitch ⅛" (3 mm) from the raw edges to stabilize the bottom of the shirt.

2   Fold the T-shirt in half, matching the shoulder seams. Press a line down the center front of the T-shirt and mark the center back at the hemline. Cut the front of the shirt open along the pressed line.

3   Refold the T-shirt in half lengthwise. Mark a point 4" (10.2 cm) down the center front opening. Mark another point at the shoulder seam next to the neckline binding. Draw a line from the shoulder mark, curving down toward the center front mark to form a scoop neckline. Cut along this line through the front fabric only, continuing around the neckline binding to the opposite side. Fold the trimmed T-shirt section to the opposite side and use as a cutting pattern. Stitch ⅛" (3 mm) from the raw edges to stabilize the neckline and front edges of the T-shirt.

4   Cut a 2" (5.1 cm) wide strip from across the bottom of the T-shirt to be used as neckline binding. Cut it open along one side.

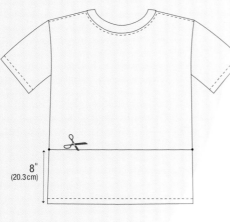

8"
(20.3 cm)

4"
(10.2 cm)

2"
(5.1 cm)   fabric strip

Construction Details

1 On the back of the T-shirt, mark 2" (5.1 cm) to the left of the center mark (refer to page 47, Step 2, Preparation). Fold the T-shirt along the hemline so that the second mark lies directly on top of the first mark, forming a pleat. Pin through all the layers of the T-shirt. Stitch across the pleat 1" (2.5 cm) above, and parallel to, the hemline.

2 Starting at the right front neckline edge, pin the grosgrain ribbon along the cut edge of the T-shirt. Fold the ribbon at the right corner, forming a miter. Continue to pin the entire hemline, miter the left hem corner, and end at the left neckline edge. Press the mitered corners.

3 Topstitch along the inside edge of the ribbon through all layers of the T-shirt and ribbon, pivoting at each corner. Carefully trim close to the stitching line, removing the T-shirt fabric from underneath the grosgrain ribbon. Topstitch the fold at both mitered corners.

4 Pin the grosgrain ribbon along the right T-shirt sleeve bottom, covering the sleeve hemline. Fold the end of the ribbon under ½" (1.3 cm), overlap the front ribbon edge, and pin to secure. Topstitch along the inside edge of the ribbon through all layers of T-shirt and ribbon. Carefully trim close to the stitching line, removing the T-shirt fabric from underneath the grosgrain ribbon. Topstitch through the ribbon ends. Repeat on the left sleeve.

5 To create the neckline binding, measure the neckline curve, starting and ending at the edge of the grosgrain ribbon. Be careful not to stretch the neckline. Subtract 3" (7.6 cm) from the neckline measurement and cut the appropriate length section from the 2" (5.1 cm) strip.

6 Fold the strip in half lengthwise, wrong sides together, and stitch each of the short ends. Turn right side out and press. Do not stretch.

7 Pin the folded strip to the neckline, starting at the left front on top of the grosgrain ribbon. Continue around the neckline edge, stretching slightly and ending at the opposite side. Stitch a ¼" (6 mm) seam through all layers. Finish the raw edges with an overcast stitch. Press.

8   Hand-stitch the snaps in place along both sides of the T-shirt front.

9   Cut the gingham ribbon in four equal pieces; trim the ends at an angle. Tie each ribbon section in a bow. Starting at the neckline edge, stitch the bows in place over the top of the snaps along the left side of the T-shirt.

10 Following the manufacturer's instructions, adhere Hot-Fix pearls to the front of the T-shirt.

t·tip

Defy the ordinary by choosing multiple widths or mixing patterns when using ribbons for your design. Sew ribbons together lengthwise; then treat as one piece of ribbon and follow instructions given above.

Aquamarine Shrug

You don't have to be a ballerina to wear this fluttery wrap shrug. Breezy cotton voile sleeves embroidered with delicate flowers provide a glamorous touch to this summer delight.

materials list:

T-shirt, aquamarine

½ yd. (0.5 m) lightweight fabric

hand-sewing needle

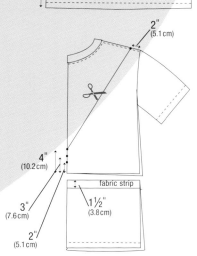

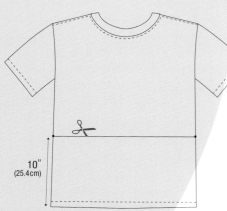

10" (25.4cm)

2" (5.1 cm)

4" (10.2cm)

3" (7.6 cm)

2" (5.1 cm)

fabric strip

1½" (3.8 cm)

T-shirt Preparation

1   Measure, then cut, 10" (25.4 cm) up from the bottom hemline *through both layers* of the T-shirt.

2   Fold the T-shirt in half, matching the shoulder seams, and press a line down the center front. Cut the front of the shirt open along the pressed line.

3   Mark a point 2" (5.1 cm) in from each sleeve along the shoulder seam. Mark a point 4" (10.2 cm) up from the bottom along both front openings. Draw a line connecting the marks from the front opening to the shoulder. Cut *only through the front* of the T-shirt.

4   Mark a point 2" (5.1 cm) below the neckline ribbing at the center back. Draw a gentle curve connecting the mark at the left shoulder to the 2" (5.1 cm) mark at the center back. Cut along this line *only through the back* of the T-shirt. Fold the trimmed T-shirt section to the right side and use as a cutting pattern.

5   Stitch ⅛" (3 mm) from the raw edges to stabilize the neckline and the front opening.

6   Cut a 1½" (3.8 cm) wide strip from the bottom of the T-shirt. Cut open along one side. This will be used for the binding.

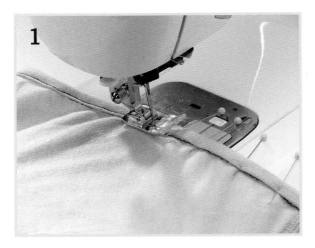

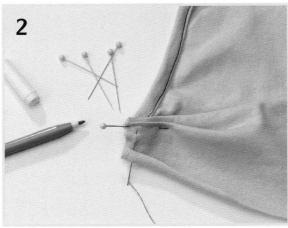

Construction Details

1 To form the neckline binding, fold the 1½" (3.8 cm) strip of T-shirt fabric in half lengthwise, wrong sides together, and press. Open and press both outside edges to the center fold. Refold and press. Open the binding and pin the right side of the binding to the inside edge of the T-shirt, starting at the bottom left hand corner. Continue pinning around the neckline to the opposite side. Stretch the binding slightly as you pin. Stitch a ⅜" (1 cm) seam. Turn the binding to the front side of the T-shirt. Topstitch through all layers of the binding and T-shirt close to the folded edges of the binding.

2 Lay the T-shirt right side up and mark points at 2" (5.1 cm) and 3" (7.6 cm) up from the bottom hemline along the 4" (10.2 cm) front using the diagram as a guide. Create a tuck by folding the fabric between the first and the second marks. Pin the folds together. Create a second tuck by folding the fabric between the first mark and the top edge, and pin the folds together. Slightly stretch the hemline, letting it roll over itself. Use a needle and thread to tack the rolled hemline over the top of the bottom front tuck. Tack the rolled hem only at the two front corners.

3 Fold the lightweight fabric in half, with the selvage edges even, and use the rotary cutter, ruler, and mat to straighten the top and the bottom edges. Cut a 1½" (3.8 cm) strip from the bottom of the fabric and set aside. Cut the remaining fabric in half along the center fold.

4 Due to the lightness of the fabric being used and the open sleeve style of this design, use a French seam to finish the inside edges of the sleeves. To create a French seam, fold the fabric in half lengthwise, wrong sides together, and stitch a ¼" (6 mm) seam. Press. Turn the sleeve right sides together and stitch a ⅜" (1 cm) seam, enclosing the ¼" (6 mm) seam. Press. Use a satin stitch on your machine to finish the bottom edge of the sleeves.

5 Sew two rows of gathering stitches along the upper edge of the fabric sleeve, ¼" (6 mm) and ½" (1.3 cm) from the edge. Turn the T-shirt wrong side out. Slide the upper edge of the fabric sleeve, wrong side out, over the bottom of the T-shirt sleeve. Pull the gathering threads and distribute the gathers evenly, as you pin the fabric over the top of the sleeve hemline. Turn the T-shirt right side out and stitch through all layers of the fabric and the T-shirt, using the hemline stitching as a guide. Repeat with the second sleeve.

6 Fold the 1½" (3.8 cm) strip of fabric in half lengthwise, right sides together. Stitch a ½" (1.3 cm) seam, forming a long tie. Turn right side out and cut in half.

7 Turn one end of the tie under ¼" (6 mm) and pin to the top of the front hemline tuck, matching the raw edges of the tie and the T-shirt. Stitch through the ends using a needle and thread; then repeat the stitching ½" (1.3 cm) from the edge of the T-shirt. Fold the tie over the top of the stitching, wrapping it around to the back. Stitch through all layers of the tie and the T-shirt to anchor. Repeat on the other side with the remaining tie. Tie an overhand knot at the end of the ties.

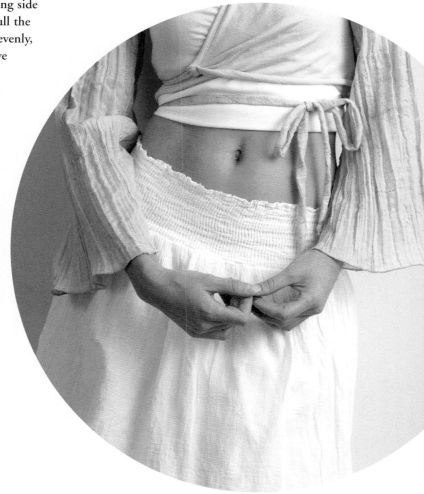

t·tip

Delicate fabrics are the best choice for this design. Consider sheer, lace, or embroidered gauze and voile for your sleeve fabric.

Oyster White Babydoll

With the addition of entredeux lace cutwork, embroidered trim, and flattering bodice ribbon ties, a plain T-shirt transforms into a look of subtle flirtation.

materials list:

T-shirt, long sleeved, oyster white

fusible web tape, 1/2" (1.3 cm) wide

entredeux trim, white, 7/16" (1.1 cm)

beading lace, white, 1" (2.5 cm) wide

ribbon, white, 1/2" (1.3 cm) wide

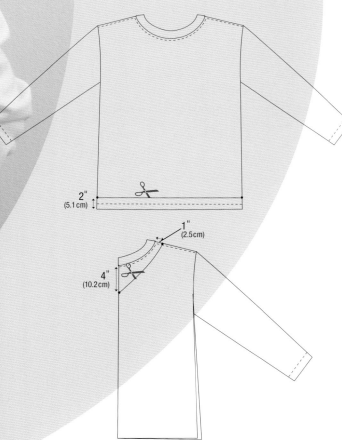

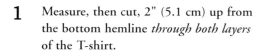

T-shirt Preparation

1 Measure, then cut, 2" (5.1 cm) up from the bottom hemline *through both layers* of the T-shirt.

2 Fold the T-shirt in half, matching the shoulder seams, and press a line down the center front. Cut the front of the shirt open along the pressed line.

3 Mark a point 4" (10.2 cm) down from the center front of the ribbed neckline. Mark points 1" (2.5 cm) out from the neckline on both shoulder seams and 1" (2.5 cm) down from the neckline at the center back. Draw a gently curving line from the right 1" (2.5 cm) mark down to the 4" (10.2 cm) mark along the center front. Cut along this line up to the shoulder; continue cutting around the back to the center mark. Fold the trimmed T-shirt section from the center back mark to the shoulder, and use the cut piece as a pattern. Use the right front as a pattern to cut the front left side.

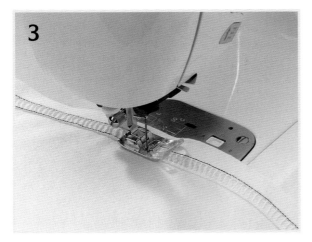

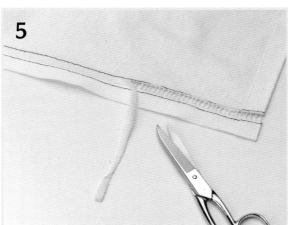

Construction Details

1. Press the fusible web tape to the wrong side of the front and the neckline edges. Remove the paper backing from the tape, turn under ½" (1.3 cm), and press.

2. Press the fusible web tape to the wrong side of the bottom hemline of the shirt. Remove the paper backing from the tape, turn under ½" (1.3 cm), and press. Topstitch along the bottom hemline of the shirt, ⅜" (1 cm) from the folded edge.

3. On the right side of the T-shirt, pin the entredeux trim to the front ½" (1.3 cm) from the edge, starting at the left side hemline and ending at the right side hemline. Topstitch along both edges of the lace.

4. Slightly stretching the width of the sleeve, pin the entredeux trim to both sleeves above the hemline. Topstitch along both edges of the trim.

5. Turn the T-shirt wrong side out and carefully trim away the fabric behind all entredeux trim.

6. To determine the placement of the beading lace, mark below the wearer's bustline and continue a placement line around the shirt. Pin the lace trim over the line. Turn the raw edges under at both ends. Topstitch through all layers along the top and bottom of the trim.

7. Thread the ribbon through the holes in the lace. Tie an overhand knot with each ribbon end.

 Note: To determine the lengths of the tape, trim, lace and ribbon, refer to **Helpful Tips for Sizing** on page 9.

t·tip

Consider using colored lace, trim, and ribbon when you create your version of this babydoll.

Mulberry Beaded Jacket

Simple lines make this jacket a must-do.
Features include a front to tie or not, beaded
accent trim, and finally a touch of glam
with the addition of randomly scattered
rhinestones and crystals.

materials list:

T-shirt, dusty purple

fusible web tape,
¼" (6 mm) wide

embroidery thread

beading needle

glass bead assortment

Hot-Fix Crystals, 3 mm,
purple and diamond

Hot-Fix heat tool

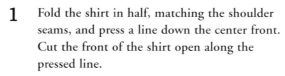

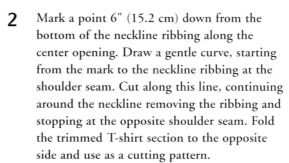

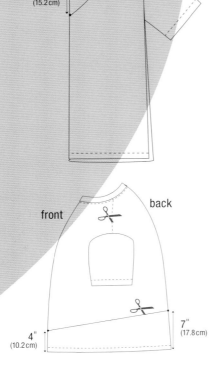

6"
(15.2 cm)

front   back

4"
(10.2 cm)

7"
(17.8 cm)

T-shirt Preparation

1 Fold the shirt in half, matching the shoulder
seams, and press a line down the center front.
Cut the front of the shirt open along the
pressed line.

2 Mark a point 6" (15.2 cm) down from the
bottom of the neckline ribbing along the
center opening. Draw a gentle curve, starting
from the mark to the neckline ribbing at the
shoulder seam. Cut along this line, continuing
around the neckline removing the ribbing and
stopping at the opposite shoulder seam. Fold
the trimmed T-shirt section to the opposite
side and use as a cutting pattern.

3 Fold the T-shirt at the back, wrong sides
together, and front openings together. Mark
a point 7" (17.8 cm) up from the bottom
hemline along the center back fold. Mark
a point 4" (10.2 cm) up from the bottom
hemline along the center front opening.
Draw a line connecting the front and back
marks. Cut along this line *through both layers*
of the T-shirt.

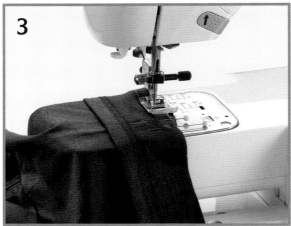

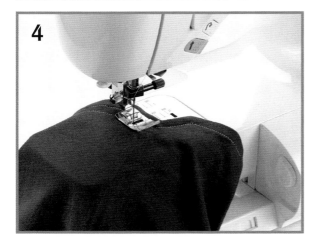

Construction Details

1 Press the fusible web tape to the wrong side of the neckline. Remove the paper backing from the tape, fold under ¼" (6 mm), and press. Repeat the procedure on the front opening edges, then the bottom hemline.

2 Refer to *Beading on Neckline Trim* on page 19. Blanket stitch along the neckline, front, and hemline edges, using three strands of embroidery thread and a beading needle, and sliding a bead onto the needle with each stitch.

3 Turn the T-shirt inside out. Fold the sleeves 2" (5.1 cm) up and press. At the center top of the sleeve place a pin 1" (2.5 cm) from the folded edge and at the fold. Mark points 1" (2.5 cm) from both sides of the pin at the fold line. Remove the center pin at the fold line. Starting at the sleeve seam, stitch a ½" (1.3 cm) seam, moving upward and stopping at the first pin. Pivot toward the pin at the center top and continue stitching. Pivot down toward the third pin; then pivot and continuing stitching around the sleeve. Remove the pins. Trim the seam allowance, cutting up into the V. Turn the T-shirt right side out and press.

4 Topstitch ⅜" (1 cm) from the bottom edge of the sleeve. Repeat, stitching two additional rows spaced ⅜" (1 cm) apart.

5 Following the manufacturer's instructions, embellish the front and sleeves of T-shirt with Hot-Fix crystals.

t·tip

Hot-Fix embellishments
are so easy.
Sprinkle the rhinestones
in a random pattern
or create a specific
design—either way they
add a classy touch
of sparkle.

Lime Sorbet

T-shirt, lime green

fusible web tape,
1/4" (6 mm) wide

embroidery needle

embroidery thread

Moda-Dea Fur Ever yarn, #3547
Limeade or any bulky weight yarn

crochet hook, US 4/E (3.5 mm)

Cool, fun, and ever so delightful. Simple single crocheting added to a blanket-stitched cropped bolero gives you life on the fringe! This design is all about the yarn.

T-shirt Preparation

1 Measure, then cut, 10" (25.4 cm) up from the bottom hemline *through both layers* of the T-shirt.

2 Fold the T-shirt in half, matching the shoulder seams, and press a line down the center front. Cut the front of the shirt open along the pressed line.

3 Mark a point 6" (15.2 cm) up from the bottom at the center front. Mark points along the bottom 6" (15.2 cm) in from the center front opening on both sides. Connect both bottom marks with the top mark. Cut along the marked lines.

4 Trim away the neckline binding along the seam.

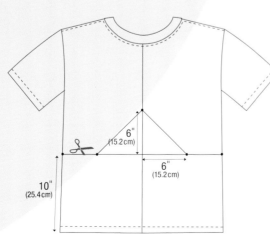

Construction Details

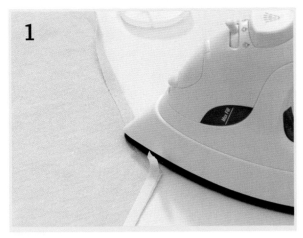

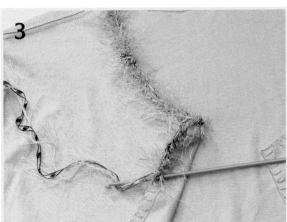

1 Press the fusible web tape to the wrong side along the neckline, the front, and the bottom edges of the T-shirt. Remove the paper backing from the tape, turn under ¼" (6 mm), and press.

2 Sew ¼" (6 mm) blanket stitches along all of the pressed edges using an embroidery needle and thread and following the instructions under *Blanket Stitch* on page 00.

3 Starting at the right shoulder seam edge and working around the T-shirt, use the crochet hook and yarn to single crochet into each blanket stitch following the instructions under *Single Crochet* on page 00.

4 Repeat with a second row of single crochet along the neckline only.

5 Crochet two 10" (25.4 cm) chains for closure ties, and attach them to the edge of the neckline.

t·tip

Combine two yarns to
achieve your perfect color.
String beads onto yarn before
crocheting; pull a bead up into
each stitch as you work. Add
more than necessary
"just in case" as extras easily
slide off when
you cut the yarn.

Vanilla Confetti

materials list:

T-shirt, white

fusible web tape, ½" (1.3 cm) wide

embroidery thread

embroidery needle

buttons, ½" (1.3 cm), assorted

A sprinkle of fun-in-the-sun confetti buttons dance across the front of this playful cropped jacket. The bright colors stand out against a warm white background.

T-SHIRT PREPARATION

1   Measure, then cut, 7" (17.8 cm) up from the bottom hemline *through both layers* of the T-shirt.

2   Fold the shirt in half, matching the shoulder seams, and press a line down the center front of the T-shirt. Cut the front of the shirt open along the pressed line.

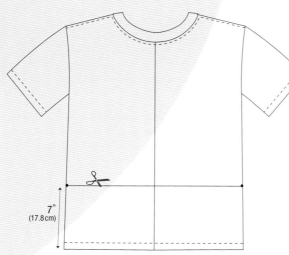

7"
(17.8 cm)

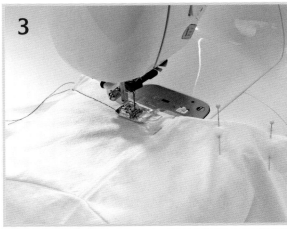

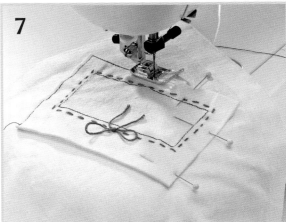

Construction Details

1   Press the fusible web tape to the wrong side of the front opening edges. Remove the paper backing from the tape, turn under ½" (1.3 cm), and press. Turn under an additional ½" (1.3 cm) and pin.

2   Press the fusible web tape to the wrong side of the bottom hemline. Remove the paper backing from the tape, turn under 1" (2.5 cm), and press. Turn under an additional 1" (2.5 cm) and pin.

3   Roll the neckline binding to the inside of the T-shirt and pin while gently stretching the binding to fit. Turn the front edges of the neckline binding under the rolled edge and pin. Topstitch through all the fabric layers along the neckline binding, approximately 1" (2.5 cm) from the top edge.

4   Topstitch through all the layers along the front opening and the bottom hemline close to the folded edge. Repeat stitching close to the outside edges. Press.

5   Turn under 1" (2.5 cm) along the sleeve hemlines and pin. Topstitch along the top and the bottom edges through all the layers. Press.

6   Cut two 6" (15.2 cm) square pockets from the excess T-shirt fabric. Press the fusible web tape to the wrong side along all sides of the pockets. Remove the paper backing from the tape, turn under ¾" (2 cm) along the side edges, and press.

7   Press the fusible web tape along the top and bottom edges. Remove the paper backing from the tape, turn the top and bottom edges under 1" (2.5 cm), and press. Topstitch close to the turned-under raw edges in the center of the pocket. Starting at the center top of the pocket, use the embroidery thread and needle to sew a decorative running stitch through all the layers of the pocket front, following the instructions under *Running Stitch* on page 15. Tie a decorative bow and cut the thread. Repeat for the other pocket. Pin the pockets at an angle onto the T-shirt front and stitch along the sides and bottom of both pockets to attach to the shirt.

8 Sew the buttons to the sleeves, the neckline, and the front of the T-shirt with the embroidery thread and needle. Attach the buttons with a simple stitch through each hole in the button and finish by tying the thread ends together.

t·tip

Dress up your button
selection with a multitude
of techniques: layer buttons
one on top of another,
use metallic or contrasting
threads, or add a bead
to each thread end
after sewing through
the button eye.

Blue Water Bolero

materials list:

T-shirt, blue

dinner plate or other circular object

1 yd. (0.92 m) fabric

hand-sewing needle

four buttons, decorative

snap fastener

transfer paper

embroidery needle

embroidery thread, rayon

Underwater colors and the soft look of ocean plant life transform a plain T-shirt into the "Blue Water Bolero." Worn on a vacation cruise or to an afternoon tea, this bolero is sure to become a wardrobe essential.

T-SHIRT PREPARATION

1 Measure, then cut, 8" (20.3 cm) up from the bottom hemline *through both layers* of the T-shirt.

2 Fold the T-shirt in half, matching the shoulder seams, and press a line down the center front. Cut the front of the shirt open along the pressed line.

3 Lay a dinner plate or other circular object on the front right side of the T-shirt, touching the bottom and the front center edge. Draw a line around the plate between the bottom and front edge. Cut along this line *through the front layer only*. Repeat on the other side of the shirt.

4 Trim away the neckline ribbing along the seam.

5 Stitch ⅛" (3 mm) from the raw edges to stabilize.

6 Remove the sleeve hems by trimming close to the stitched hemlines.

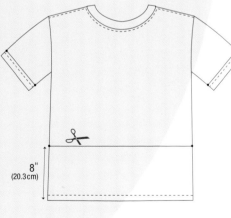

8"
(20.3cm)

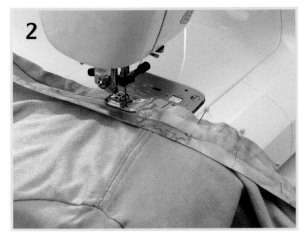

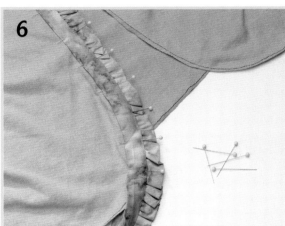

Construction Details, Bolero

1 Create the double-sided bias binding ruffle and the bias binding following the instructions under *Sewing* on pages 12 and 14.

2 Starting and ending at the front neckline edge, pin a section of the bias binding to the T-shirt, right sides together. Stitch a ½" (1.3 cm) seam. Fold the bias binding to the inside of the neckline and hand-stitch along the inside seam line.

3 Pin a section of the binding to the shirt sleeve, right sides together, starting and ending at the underarm seam line. Overlap the binding ends. Stitch a ½" (1.3 cm) seam. Fold the bias binding to the inside of the sleeve and hand-stitch to the inside seam line.

4 Cut a 10" (25.4 cm) section of the bias binding in half along the center fold line. Fold in half lengthwise, right sides together, and stitch a ¼" (6 mm) seam. Turn right side out and cut into two pieces. Form two loops. Lay one loop across the other to form a bow at the binding. Center a button on top of the loops and sew through all the layers.

5 Remove approximately ½" (1.3 cm) of stitches at both ends of the bias ruffle, fold the raw edges under, and press.

6 Slide the bias ruffle trim over the front opening of the T-shirt, starting at the top edge. Pin the ruffle around the bottom and up the opposite side of the T-shirt. Stitch close to the folded edge.

7 Sew a snap fastener at the neckline.

8 Use the transfer paper to transfer the stitching lines to the front of the T-shirt.

9 Use two strands of rayon embroidery thread and chain stitch along the pattern lines, following the instructions under *Embroidery* on page 15.

10 Press the embroidery carefully.

Organic form embroidery creates a look of fine fabric. Try your hand at creating your own pattern for embroidery. A simple doodle can easily be transformed into a unique embellishment.

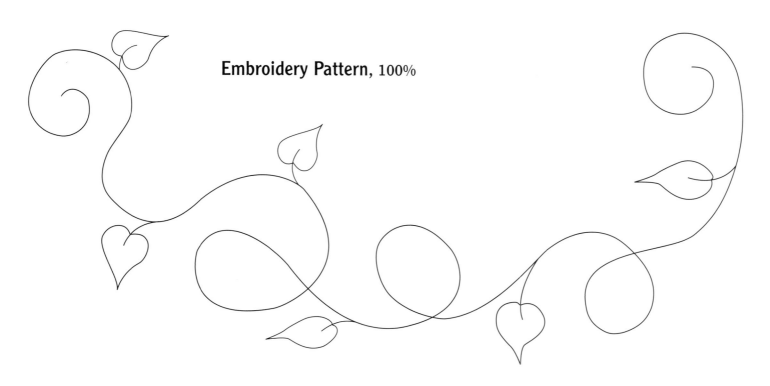

Embroidery Pattern, 100%

Construction Details,
Bolero Back Tab Tie

1 Cut two 8" (20.3 cm) sections of the bias strip. Fold the ends to the inside and press. Topstitch through all the layers along both edges of the bias strip.

2 Measure 4" (10.2 cm) up from the bottom edge of the T-shirt, and pin to mark the center back.

3 Lay a ruler parallel to the bottom hemline at the 4" (10.2 cm) pin. Place pins 3" (7.6 cm) from the pin on both sides. Remove the center pin.

4 Fold one edge of a bias strip over ½" (1.3 cm) and press. Pin the bias strip over each pin mark, with the folded edge facing away from the center. Topstitch over the bias strip end. Repeat at the other side.

5 Sew a button on top of the stitching and tie the ends together in an overhand knot.

Terrific T-shirt Remixes

A bit of embellishment takes
a simple T-shirt from
spartan to special.
Grommets and bias tape,
paint and ribbon, fabric
and trim—all tiny touches
that add big impact.

Retro Sunset

materials list:

T-shirt, orange

½ yd. (0.5 m) fabric

hand-sewing needle

Simple fabric manipulation creates an interesting hemline, pocket, and neckline accent. Known to quilters as a prairie-point or saw-tooth trim, this enhancement works perfectly on a T-shirt.

 T-shirt Preparation

1   Measure, then cut, 4" (10.2 cm) up from the bottom hemline *through both layers* of the T-shirt.

2   Stitch ⅛" (3 mm) from the raw edges to stabilize the bottom of the shirt.

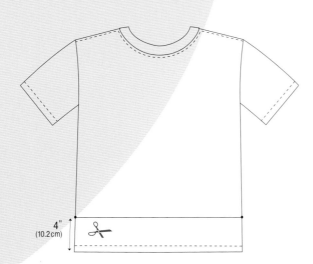

4"
(10.2 cm)

Construction Details

1 Cut approximately eighty 2" (5.1 cm) squares from the fabric. The number of squares needed will vary depending on the size of the T-shirt. Following the instructions under *Sewing* on page 13 create the prairie-point trim.

2 Beginning at the center back, pin a section of the prairie-point trim along the neckline of the T-shirt, butting the raw edge up to the neckline binding seam line. Cut the stitches of the first prairie-point to open the fold; then insert the last prairie-point for a well-finished look. Baste in place.

3 Roll the neckline binding to the front of the T-shirt, covering the raw edges of trim; hand-stitch in place, covering the basting stitches.

4 Matching the raw edge to the T-shirt bottom, pin the prairie-point trim to the right side of the T-shirt starting at the center back. Beginning at the center back and with the right sides together, pin a section of the prairie-point trim along the bottom edge of the T-shirt. Cut the stitches of the first prairie-point to open its fold; then insert the last prairie-point into the opening. Stitch a ¼" (6 mm) seam. Turn the stitching to the inside of the T-shirt and press. Finish the raw edges with an overcast stitch.

Alternating two or more print fabric prairie-points gives a very different look. Add beads to the point ends around the neckline for even more pizzazz.

Construction Details, Pockets

1 Cut two 8" × 5½" (20.3 × 14 cm) rectangles of fabric. With right sides together, fold each piece in half to measure 4" × 5½" (10.2 × 14 cm). Stitch along all raw edges, leaving a 2" (5.1 cm) opening.

2 Turn right side out and hand-stitch the opening closed. Cut a section of the prairie-point trim to fit the bottom of the pocket edge. Fold the points of the end triangles under to fit, if necessary. Pin, and then stitch, the trim to the underside of the pocket bottom.

3 Turn the prairie-point trim and press. Pin the pockets in place 1½" (3.8 cm) up from the bottom edge of the T-shirt, centering the pockets evenly. Topstitch through all the layers along the sides and bottom edges of the pockets.

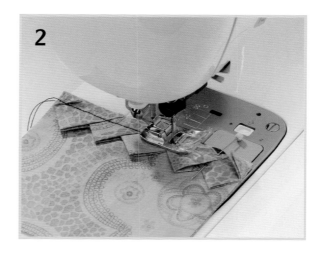

Caribbean Ribbons

materials list:

T-shirt, blue

grosgrain ribbon, 3/8" (1 cm) wide

assorted grosgrain ribbons,
1" (2.5 cm) wide

Hot-Fix nail heads,
blue/green diamond

Hot-Fix applicator tool

Complementary grosgrain ribbons
provide a framework for this cropped
design. Drama is created by the addition
of Hot-Fix nail-head accents.

T-shirt Preparation

1 Measure, then cut, 9" (23 cm) up from the
   bottom hemline *through both layers* of the
   T-shirt. Stitch 1/8" (3 mm) from the raw edges
   to stabilize the bottom.

2 Fold the T-shirt in half, matching the
   shoulder seams, and press a line down the
   center front of the T-shirt. Open the T-shirt
   and place marks 3" (7.6 cm) and 5" (12.7 cm)
   up from the bottom hemline along the center
   fold. Mark points along the bottom hem,
   3" (7.6 cm) from the center fold line on
   both sides. These marks will be used for
   the ribbon placement.

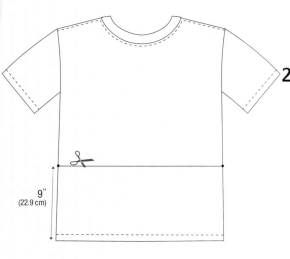

9"
(22.9 cm)

5"
(12.7cm)

3"
(7.6cm)

3"
(7.6cm)

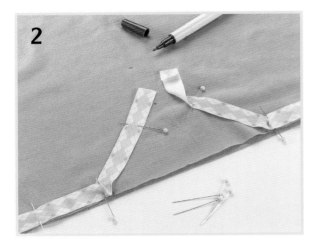

Construction Details

1   Place the ribbon ½" (1.3 cm) above the center 3" (7.6 cm) mark, and angled toward the left bottom 3" mark; then pin. Just above the hemline turn the ribbon, mitering the turn so the bottom edge rests along the bottom of the hemline. Continue to pin the ribbon around the bottom of the T-shirt, miter at the opposite 3" (7.6 cm) mark, and angle toward the beginning mark. Trim the ribbon end ½" (1.3 cm) longer than needed, turn the raw edge under, and pin in place. Topstitch along the top edge of the ribbon.

2   Turn the T-shirt wrong side out and carefully trim along the stitching line, removing the T-shirt fabric from underneath the grosgrain ribbon.

3   Topstitch the mitered corners.

4   Repeat step 1 with a second ribbon, placing it above and touching the top edge of the first ribbon. Topstitch along both edges of the ribbon and the mitered corners.

5   Starting at the 5" (12.7 cm) mark, pin the narrow grosgrain ribbon parallel to the second ribbon, leaving an even width between them. Miter the ribbon at the turns.

6   Cut two 3" (7.56 cm) pieces of ribbon for the decorative tabs. Tuck the tabs under the pinned mitered corners. They will extend over the mitered corners of the first two ribbons and below the ribbon hemline.

7   Stitch along the top and bottom edges of the narrow ribbon and the mitered corners. Fold the ends of the ribbon tabs under so they only extend ½" (1.3 cm) past the ribbon hemline. Topstitch the fold at the hemline and the tabs along both long edges.

Designer Extra, Watchband

1 Cut a 1½" (3.8 cm) strip from the bottom of the T-shirt. Cut in half and pull the strips taut, creating tubes.

2 Measure your wrist and cut a piece of narrow grosgrain ribbon and the fabric tubes this length.

3 To create the watchband, thread the tubes and ribbon through ⅜" (1 cm) rings inserted at both sides of the watch face.

4 Sew the ribbon and tubes together at each end by hand. Sew a decorative ring (toggle clasp) to one end and a closing bar to the other.

fashion t-shirts

Midnight Seas

materials list:

T-shirt, navy

bias tape, 1" (2.5 cm) wide

twenty-eight grommets

grommet setter

hammer

leather cording

seventeen pony beads

Here's a clever take on yacht club fashion. Whether you sail the high seas or simply picnic at your favorite lakeside park, you'll enjoy both comfort and style while sporting this design. Silver grommets and leather cording add just the right amount of character to a simple navy T-shirt.

 T-shirt Preparation

1 Mark a line 1" (2.5 cm) down from the bottom of the ribbed neckline binding. Cut along this line, removing the neckline binding.

2 Stitch ⅛" (3 mm) from the raw edges to stabilize the neckline.

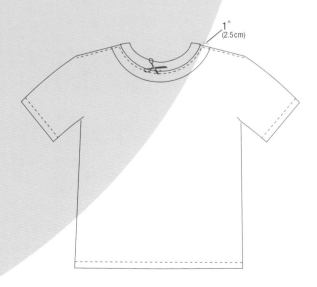

1" (2.5 cm)

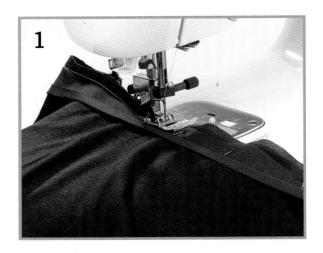

Construction Details

1 Open the folds of the bias tape. Pin the bias tape to the T-shirt along the neckline edge, right sides together, starting at a shoulder seam. Turn the raw edges of the bias tape under ½" (1.3 cm) and overlap. Stitch in the fold of the tape.

2 Turn the bias tape to the inside of the T-shirt and press. Topstitch along the top and the bottom edges of the bias tape, through all layers of the T-shirt and bias tape.

3 Lay the T-shirt wrong side up. Along the side seam, mark a point 1" (2.5 cm) below the wearer's natural waistline. Repeat on the other side.

4 Draw a line to join the marks in front and in back. Pin the top edge of the bias tape along this line. Fold the raw edges under and overlap the ends. Stitch along the top and the bottom edges of the bias tape.

Cord and Beads

1 Cut two 12" (30.5 cm) sections of leather cording. Thread a piece of the cording through the grommets on the sleeves. Add a bead to each end and tie with overhand knots.

2 Starting at the center front of the neckline, thread cording through the grommets, stopping at the center back grommet. Add a bead, thread the cording back through the center, and then continue threading the cording through the remaining neckline grommets. Trim the cording, leaving a 10" (25.4 cm) tie on both sides. Add three beads to each end and tie with overhand knots.

3 Starting at the front of the T-shirt, thread the cording around the waistline. Trim the cording, leaving a 12" (30.5 cm) tie on both sides. Add three beads to each cord end and tie overhand knots.

With the wide variety of grommet colors and the wide array of cording available today, your design can take on a number of looks. Striped shoelaces provide an interesting contrast.

Grommet Placement

1 Place pins as indicated in the instructions for neckline, waistline, and sleeves to mark the placement of the grommets.

2 Snip a small X at each pin placement.

3 Set a grommet in each X, following the manufacturer's instructions.

Neckline

1 Mark the center front and center back of the T-shirt neckline on the bias tape with a straight pin. Place a pin on the bias tape 1" (2.5 cm) from the right shoulder seam at the front neckline.

2 Measure the distance between this pin and the front center pin, and place another pin halfway between the first two pins. Repeat the pinning on the left front; then repeat again on both sides of the back neckline.

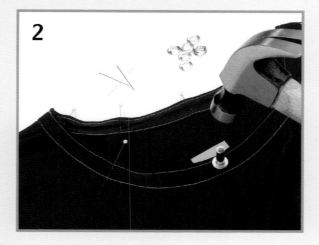

Waistline

1 Mark the center front waistline of the T-shirt with a pin. Place a second pin 1" (2.5 cm) to the right of the center pin. Mark the right side of the T-shirt with a third pin.

2 Measure the distance between the second and third pins. Divide the measurement by three. Place a pin the resultant distance away from both the second pin and the third pin. Repeat on the other side of the waistline; then remove the centermost pin.

3 Measure the distance between the two side pins across the back of the T-shirt and divide by seven. Use this measurement to mark the placement of six additional pins.

Sleeves

1 Mark the center of the sleeve at the hemline with a pin. Place additional pins 1¼" (3.2 cm) from both sides of the pin. Remove the center pin.

Tricolor Tropical

materials list:

T-shirt, sea green

fusible web tape,
1/2" (1.3 cm) wide

hand-sewing needle

embroidery thread

embroidery needle

eleven sequins, dangling shell

Dangling shell sequins add a delicate touch to a simple design. Construction details create interest while sewing is kept to a minimum.

 T-shirt Preparation

1   Measure, then cut, 3" (7.6 cm) up from the hemline *through both layers* of the T-shirt. The 3" (7.6 cm) strip will be used to create the front placket.

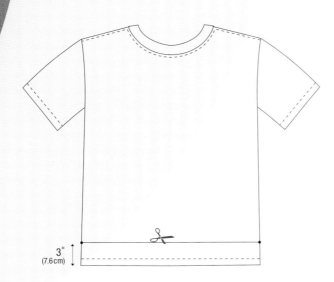

3"
(7.6 cm)

Construction Details

1 Press the fusible web tape to the wrong side of the T-shirt along the hemline. Remove the paper backing from the tape, turn under 1" (2.5 cm), and press. Turn under an additional 1" (2.5 cm) and pin. Topstitch the hemline through all layers close to the folded edge.

2 Cut open the 3" (7.6 cm) strip of T-shirt fabric along one side. Press fusible web tape to the wrong side down the center. Remove the paper backing from the tape, fold the left edge of the strip over the fusible tape, and press.

3 Fold the opposite edge toward the center and press. Press the fusible web tape to the edge of the strip. Cut a 10" (25. cm) section from the strip, and set it aside to be used as the sleeve tabs.

4 Remove the paper backing from the tape and place the strip down the center front of the T-shirt, butting the top edge to the neckline seam. Fold the bottom edge to the wrong side of the T-shirt; trim any excess fabric. Turn the raw end under and press the entire placket. Topstitch through all layers, ¼" (6 mm) from both edges.

5 Roll the neckline binding toward the right side of the T-shirt, covering the neckline seam line and the front placket. Hand-stitch in place around the neckline.

6 To create the sleeve tabs, cut the 10" (25.4) section into two 5" pieces. Turn the ends under and pin. Topstitch through all layers, ¼" (6 mm) from both edges. Fold the tab in half and slide it over the sleeve hemline at the top of the sleeve. Using the embroidery thread and needle, stitch through all layers, attaching a shell button to the top of the tab on the sleeve. This also secures the tab to the T-shirt.

7 Sew the shell buttons to the front neckline using the embroidery thread and needle. Tie the thread ends together at the front.

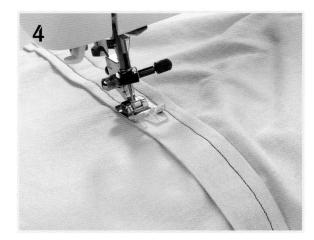

t·tip

To enhance the illusion
created by the faux
placket, accent with
buttonholes
and buttons.

Scarlet Flower

materials list:

T-shirt, long sleeved, red

transfer paper

pencil

fusible bias tape, 1/4" (6 mm) wide

The clean graphic lines of stained glass leading provide a bold fashion statement. Prefolded bias tape with a fusible adhesive backing makes this project quick and easy to do.

Construction Details

1 Enlarge the Scarlet Flowers pattern on page 95 by 200 percent using a copy machine. Lay the T-shirt right side up. Center the pattern on the top of the T-shirt and pin in place at the corners. Slide the transfer paper between the pattern and the T-shirt (check to ensure the transfer side is next to the T-shirt). Firmly trace over the pattern lines with the pencil to transfer the design to the T-shirt. You will need to slide the transfer paper around under the pattern to copy the entire design onto the T-shirt.

2 Fuse the bias tape in place, following the numerical order listed on the pattern. This allows you to cover raw edges as you work. Stitch along both edges of the tape.

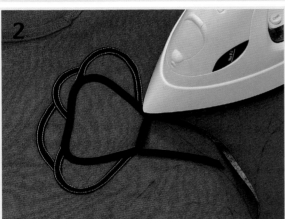

t·tip

Enhance a T-shirt with your favorite stained glass design. Add pizzazz and the look of stained glass by cutting fabric to fit within the sections of "leading."

Embroidery Pattern, enlarge 200%

Coral Floral

materials list:

T-shirt, coral

¹/₂ yd. (0.5 m) or one
fat quarter of floral
print fabric

fusible web tape,
¹/₂" (1.3 cm) wide

fabric marker

piece of paper

masking tape

scrap cardboard

craft knife

acrylic paint, assorted colors

sponge brush

fabric paint medium

embroidery thread

embroidery needle

glass beads

two buttons

This design features multiple textures
created through the clever use of fabric,
paint, and beading. Your choice of fabric
will lead the way when choosing
paint colors.

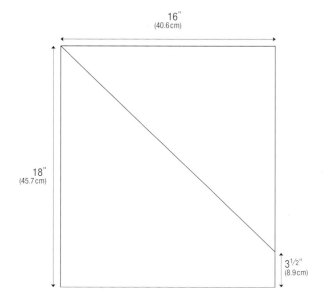

16"
(40.6 cm)

18"
(45.7 cm)

3¹/₂"
(8.9 cm)

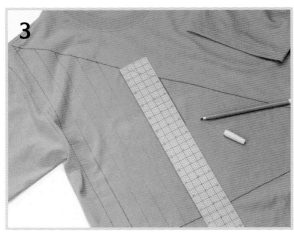

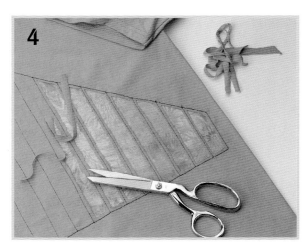

Construction Details

1 Draw an 18" × 16" (46 × 40.5 cm) rectangle on the back of the floral print fabric. Mark a point 2½" (6.4 cm) up from the bottom right edge along the 18" (46 cm) length. Draw a line from the mark to the top left corner. Cut along the lines. Finish all raw edges with an overcast stitch. Press the fusible web tape to the right side of the fabric along all edges.

2 Turn the T-shirt inside out and lay it on a flat surface, with the front side of the T-shirt facing up. Remove the paper backing from the fusible web tape, and place the fabric right side down, with the point at the shoulder seam and the bottom parallel to the T-shirt hemline. Press to secure the fabric to the T-shirt. Stitch all sides close to the edge.

3 Turn the T-shirt right side out. Draw vertical lines 1" (2.5 cm) apart using a ruler and fabric marker. Topstitch through the T-shirt front and the fabric along all lines

Note: If necessary, adjust the width of the lines to keep them evenly spaced. Be sure to keep the lines running vertically.

4 Carefully trim the fabric from between the stitching lines.

5 Lay a piece of paper on top of a fabric scrap and trace around a chosen pattern detail. Enlarge the traced design 200 percent, and then an additional 64 percent using a copy machine. Tape the design onto a piece of thin cardboard.

Note: You may enlarge the design element to any size that works with the size of T-shirt you are using.

6 Cut out the design elements using a craft knife. Be sure to leave areas or bridges between the design elements.

7 Refer to the instructions under *Stamping and Stenciling* on page 21 and use the cardboard stencil to create the stenciled motif along the slanted edge of the cutwork.

8 Stitch beads on top of the painted design where desired, using the embroidery thread and needle.

9 Cut two 1½" × 18" (3.8 × 46 cm) strips of fabric. Fold the strips in half lengthwise and press open. Fold the edges to the center fold, and press. Fold in half; then stitch along the open edge. Cut both strips into two pieces.

10 Place a pin 3" (7.6 cm) up from the center top edge of the sleeve. Turn the raw ends of the fabric strips over ¼" (6 mm). Pin the end of one strip to the outside and the other end to the inside of the sleeve at the pin mark. Set a button on top and stitch through all layers, attaching the ties and the button. Tie a bow gathering up the sleeve hemline. Repeat with the second sleeve.

t·tip

Let the fabric shine by choosing complementary colors of paint and beads.

Toddlers to Tikes
T Designs

Bright and happy
designs with special little
extras are sure to make any
little girl all smiles. Use her
favorite colors and themes to
personalize the designs and
win thank-you hugs.

Bubblegum Gingham

materials list:

T-shirt, pink,
youth small (6/8)

1/2 yd. (0.5 m) gingham fabric

dinner plate or other circular object

bias tape maker, 1/2" (1.3 cm)

button

paper plate

acrylic paint, white

fabric painting medium

paintbrush

safety pin

Pink and white—two hues coloring little girls' dreams. Decorative stitching and playful dots add just the right touch to this sweet—treat tee and swingy purse.

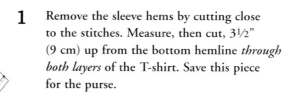

T-shirt Preparation

1 Remove the sleeve hems by cutting close to the stitches. Measure, then cut, 3½" (9 cm) up from the bottom hemline *through both layers* of the T-shirt. Save this piece for the purse.

2 Fold the shirt in half, matching the shoulder seams, and press a line down the center front of the T-shirt. Cut the front of the shirt open along the pressed line.

3 Lay a dinner plate or other circular object on the front right side of the T-shirt, touching the bottom and the front center edge. Draw a line around the plate between the bottom and front edge. Cut along this line *through the front layer only*. Repeat on the other side of the shirt.

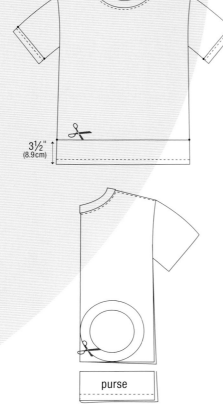

3½"
(8.9cm)

purse

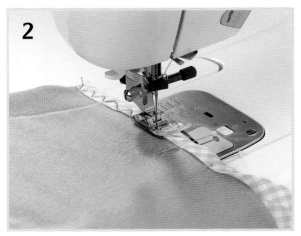

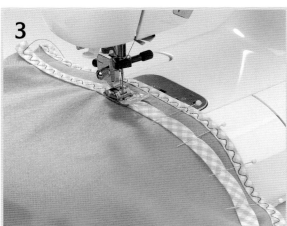

Construction Details

1 Refer to *Sewing* on page 12 to create the gingham bias tape.

2 Turn the raw edges of the bias tape under and press. Slip the bias tape over the cut edges of the T-shirt (omit the neckline), pin in place, and stitch, using a decorative machine stitch.

3 Lay the gingham bias tape on top of the T-shirt, pinning it parallel to and ½" (1.3 cm) away from the first bias tape. Topstitch though all layers of bias and the T-shirt using a decorative stitch.

4 Turn the ends of the bias tape under and press. With 2½" (6.4 cm) of bias tape extending beyond the left side of the neckline, slip the bias tape over the neckline and pin.

5 Fold the extended section of bias tape in half lengthwise and topstitch. Fold the section back toward the neckline and pin.

6 Topstitch through all the layers of neckline binding tape using a decorative stitch. This will secure the button loop.

7 Sew the button to the inner gingham bias tape on the right side, 1¼" (3.2 cm) down from the top of the neckline.

8 Squeeze a small amount of paint and fabric painting medium onto a paper plate and mix. Refer to the manufacturer's instructions when measuring paint and medium. Randomly add dots to the front and back of the T-shirt using the handle of a paintbrush.

Designer Extra, Poof Purse

What little girl doesn't love to carry her favorite items with her everywhere?

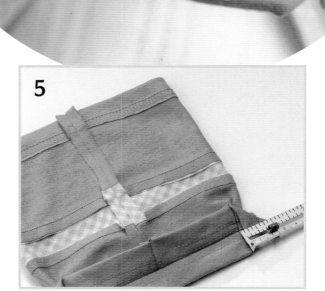

1   Cut the 3½" (9 cm) section vertically into two pieces.

2   Measure the length of one piece and cut a 1" (2.5 cm) wide length of gingham fabric this length.

3   With right sides together, pin the gingham strip along the top of one piece. Stitch a ¼" (6 mm) seam. Press the seam toward the gingham fabric. Stitch the second piece to the opposite edge of the gingham strip.

4   Fold the sewn piece in half, right sides together, and stitch, forming a tube with the gingham strip in the middle.

5   Fold the tube in half, centering the seam line at the back. Close the bottom edge by stitching just above the T-shirt hemline stitching. Press the bottom seam open. Measure ¾" (1.9 cm) in from both points; then draw a line perpendicular to the bottom seam line. Stitch along this line. Repeat on the other side. Turn the purse right side out.

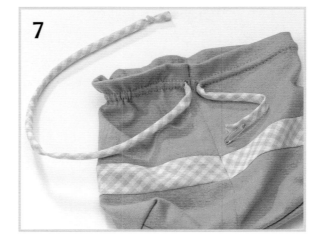

6   Cut a 1" × 32" (2.5 × 81.5 cm) strip of gingham fabric. Fold in half lengthwise, right sides together. Stitch a ¼" (6 mm) seam. Turn right side out. Cut 6" (15.2 cm) from the end and set aside.

7   Cut a vertical slit ¼" (6 mm) from the seam line through the top fabric layer between the two lines of T-shirt hemline stitching. Repeat the cut on the other side of the seam line. Thread the tie through the slit, coming out on the opposite side, using a safety pin attached to one end of the tie. Tie overhand knots at the ends of the ties.

8   Tie a bow with the 6" (15.2 cm) section of gingham fabric. Stitch to the front of the purse.

9   Paint the dots following Step 8 under *Construction Details* for the T-shirt.

Sunshine Friends

Colorful bugs and butterflies flitter and flutter every which way. This delightful shirt is sure to wing its way into a little girl's heart.

materials list:

T-shirt, yellow, youth small (6/8)

hand-sewing needle

½ yd. (0.5 m) fabric

one button, large flower

three buttons, bumblebees

 ## T-shirt Preparation

1   Measure, then cut, 6" (15.2 cm) up from the bottom hemline *through both layers* of the T-shirt.

2   Stitch ⅛" (3 mm) from the raw edges to stabilize the bottom of the shirt.

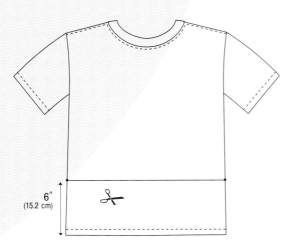

6"
(15.2 cm)

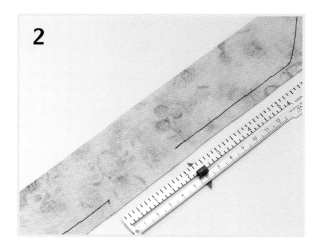

Construction Details, Shirt

1 Measure the bottom hemline of the T-shirt and add 1" (2.5 cm). Cut a strip of fabric 4" (10.2 cm) by the measurement. Fold the strip in half lengthwise, wrong sides together, and press. Turn under ½" (1.3 cm) along the length of one edge. Press. With right sides together, stitch the short ends together. Press the seam open. Open the band and pin the T-shirt hemline right sides together, matching the seam line to the center front of the T-shirt. Stitch a ½" (1.3 cm) seam. Press. Encase the bottom seam by turning the band to the wrong side of the T-shirt; hand-stitch in place along the seam.

2 Sew a gathering stitch through the center seam line of the hemline accent using a thread and needle. Pull the threads taut to gather the fabric, and stitch to anchor the threads.

Construction Details, Tie

1 Cut a 4" × 15" (10.2 × 38 cm) strip of fabric. Fold in half lengthwise, right sides together. Stitch along all open edges, leaving a 2" (5.1 cm) opening, using the photo as a guide.

2 Trim away the excess fabric. Turn right side out and press. Handstitch the opening closed. Tie, using an overhand knot. Hand-stitch to the front of the T-shirt.

Add contrasting piping or rickrack to the pocket and sleeve tabs for visual zing. Let the fabric, buttons, or trims inspire you!

Construction Details, Pocket and Flap

Pocket

1   Cut a 7" (17.8 cm) square of fabric for the pocket. Fold under the sides and bottom edges of the pocket ½" (1.3 cm), and press. Turn under the top edge of the pocket ½" (1.3 cm), and press. Unfold the top edge, then turn the raw edge in to meet the fold line; press again. Refold the edge and stitch along the fold. Center the pocket on the front of the T-shirt. Topstitch the sides and bottom close to the edge. Topstitch a second row ¼" (6 mm) from the first stitching line.

Pocket Flap

1   Cut a 6" × 7" (15.2 × 17.8 cm) strip of fabric. Fold in half lengthwise, right sides together. Place a mark 1" (2.5 cm) up from the bottom on both side edges. Mark the center along the bottom edge. Draw a line from the center mark to both corners.

2   Stitch on the marked line, leaving a 2" (5.1 cm) opening along one of the edges. Trim away excess fabric. Turn right side out and press. Hand-stitch the opening closed.

3   Topstitch the sides and bottom close to the edge. Topstitch a second row ¼" (6 mm) from the first stitch line.

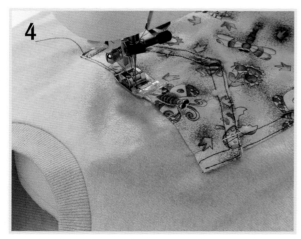

4   Center the pocket flap over the pocket and stitch along the top edge close to the fold. Topstitch a second row ¼" (6 mm) from the first stitching.

5   Stitch the daisy and a bee button in place on the pocket flap.

Construction Details, Sleeve Tabs

1   1. Cut a 4" × 8" (10.2 × 20.3 cm) strip of fabric. Fold the strip in half lengthwise, right sides together, and stitch a ¼" (6 mm) seam along the long edge.

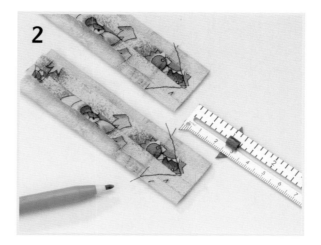

2   Press flat, keeping the seam line in the center. Cut into two 4" (10.2 cm) lengths. Draw a line 1" (2.5 cm) up from one end of the tab. Draw a V as indicated by the photo. Stitch the point at the end of the strip.

3   Turn the tab right side out and press the flat end under ½" (1.3 cm). Pin the tab to the center of the sleeve bottom. Stitch in place.

4   Sew a bee button to the top of the tab, stitching through the T-shirt. Repeat with the other tab.

Lemon Drop Celebration

Every little girl enjoys feeling special on her birthday! Create a one-of-a-kind wearable birthday card for your little one.

materials list:

T-shirt, yellow,
youth small (6/8)

¼ yd. (0.25 m) fabric, print

¼ yd. (0.25 m) fabric,
coordinating print

hand-sewing needle

fusible web sheet

1 yd. (0.92 m) grosgrain ribbon,
red, ³⁄₈" (1 cm) wide

24" (61 cm) grosgrain ribbon, green,
³⁄₈" (1cm) wide

12" (30.5 cm) grosgrain ribbon,
white, 1" (2.5 cm) wide

fusible web tape, ¼" (6 mm)
and ½" (1.3 cm) wide

T-shirt Preparation

1 Measure, then cut, 2" (5.1 cm) up from the bottom hemline *through both layers* of the T-shirt.

2 Fold the T-shirt in half, matching the shoulder seams. Place a pin 2" (5.1 cm) up from the bottom hemline along the side of the T-shirt. Draw a gentle curve down from the pin to the hemline. Cut along the drawn line *through all layers* of the T-shirt. Stitch ⅛" (3 mm) from the raw edges to stabilize the bottom of the shirt.

3 Remove sleeve hems by trimming close to the stitched hemlines.

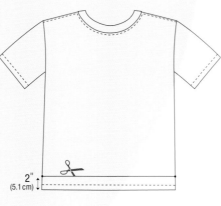

2"
(5.1cm)

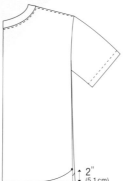

2"
(5.1cm)

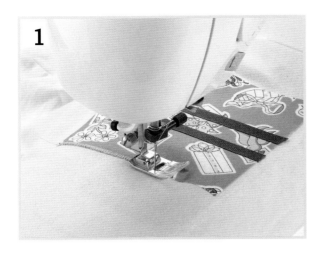

Construction Details

1 Begin by creating the decorative packages. Press the fusible web sheet to the wrong side of the coordinating fabric. Cut a 5" (12.7 cm) square, a 4" (10.2 cm) square, and a 5" × 4" (12.7 × 10.2 cm) rectangle. Remove the paper backing from the fusible web on the 5" (12.7 cm) square, place it face-up on the front of the T-shirt, and press. Cut two 5" (12.7 cm) pieces of red grosgrain ribbon, and press fusible tape to the backs. Remove the paper backing from the tape and press the ribbons on top of the fabric square, approximately ⅜" (1 cm) apart. Finish the raw edges around the square in a satin stitch.

2 Place the other two packages, overlapping the first package slightly, and press. Decorate one with a 5" (12.7 cm) length of white grosgrain ribbon and the other with two 4" (10.2 cm) lengths of green grosgrain ribbon placed crosswise to each other. Secure all edges with a satin stitch.

3 Cut two 2" × 45" (5.1 × 115 cm) strips of fabric. With right sides together, stitch the strips together along the short ends, forming a circle. Press the seams open. Finish one edge of the circle with a decorative stitch. Sew two rows of gathering stitches along the opposite edge, ¼" (6 mm) and ⅛" (3 mm) from edge.

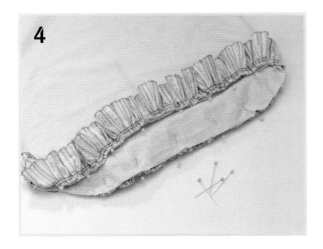

4 Pin the seams of the circle to the sides of the T-shirt bottom, right sides together. Pull the gathering threads and distribute the gathers around the bottom of the T-shirt. Stitch a ¼" (6 mm) seam. Finish the raw edges with an overcast stitch and press the ruffle down from the bottom of the T-shirt.

5 Measure the circumference of the cut edge of the sleeve and add 1" (2.5 cm). Cut two strips of fabric 2" (5.1 cm) by this measurement. Press a strip in half lengthwise, wrong sides together. Open and fold the raw edges to the center fold, creating a binding. Stitch the strip together along the short ends, right sides together, using a ½" (1.3 cm) seam. Open the folded binding and pin the binding to the cut edge of the sleeve, right sides together. Stitch a ½" (1.3 cm) seam through all layers. Press the binding down from the T-shirt sleeve and wrap it around to the underside of the sleeve. Hand-stitch the binding to the inside edge of the T-shirt sleeve along the seam line. Repeat for the second sleeve.

6 Tie or loop red, green, and white ribbons to create the bows and hand-stitch to the top of the packages.

t·tip

Time flies and little ones grow fast. Mark those special occasions with a unique T-shirt. Consider using an oversized shirt and creating a birthday sleepover tee. Be prepared—chances are her friends will want one for their birthdays too!

Flower Power

The simple construction of this cropped jacket is highlighted by fun crocheted trim and flower accents.

T-shirt, blue, youth small (6/8)

fabric marker

fusible web tape, ¼" (6 mm) wide

embroidery needle

one skein DMC 5 pearl cotton, red

one skein Aunt Lydia's® Beadies crochet yarn, #0038 Surfer or any medium weight yarn

crochet hook, US 2/C (2.75 mm)

fabric glue

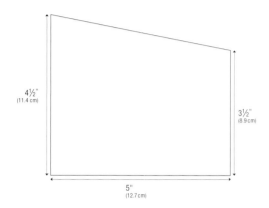

4½" (11.4 cm)

3½" (8.9 cm)

5" (12.7 cm)

2" (5.1 cm)

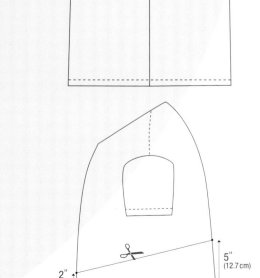

5" (12.7 cm)

2" (5.1 cm)

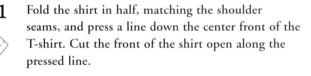

T-shirt Preparation

1 Fold the shirt in half, matching the shoulder seams, and press a line down the center front of the T-shirt. Cut the front of the shirt open along the pressed line.

2 Mark a point 2" (5.1 cm) down from the bottom of the neckline ribbing on one side of the center opening. Draw a gentle curve from the mark to the shoulder seam neck ribbing. Cut along this line and continue around the neckline, stopping at the opposite shoulder seam. Fold the T-shirt cut section to the front and use as a cutting pattern.

3 Fold the T-shirt in half along the center back, wrong sides together, and match the front openings. Mark a point 5" (12.7 cm) up from the bottom hemline along the center back fold. Mark a point 2" (5.1 cm) up from the bottom hemline along the center front opening. Draw a line connecting the front and center back markings. Cut along this line *through both layers* of the T-shirt.

4 Cut two 5" (12.7 cm) squares using the fabric removed from the bottom of the T-shirt. Set aside for making the pockets.

Construction Details, shirt

1   Press fusible web tape to the wrong side of the neckline and the front opening edges. Remove the paper backing from the tape, turn under ¼" (6 mm), and press. Repeat along the hemline.

2   Blanket stitch along the neckline, front, and hemline edges using pearl cotton and an embroidery needle, and following the instruction under *Blanket Stitch* on page 15.

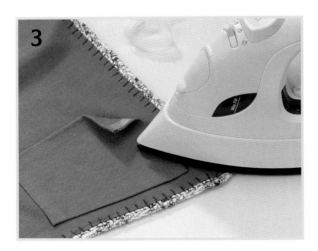

3   Cut the two 5" (12.7 cm) squares of pocket fabric on an angle, using the photo as a guide. Press fusible web tape to the wrong side of all edges. Remove the paper backing from the tape, turn the fabric ¼" (6 mm) under, and press. Press fusible tape to the underside of the side and bottom edges. Remove the paper backing from the tape, and press the pockets to the front of the T-shirt.

4   Stitch an X at the top corners of both of the pockets using the pearl cotton and an embroidery needle.

5   Single crochet into the blanket stitch around the neckline, front, and hemline edges using the crochet yarn, and following the instruction under *Single Crochet* on page 17.

6   Crochet two chain-stitch ties and attach them to the front of the T-shirt.

Construction Details, Flowers

1   Crochet an eight-stitch chain with the crochet yarn; then join to the first stitch, creating a petal. Crochet four more petals to create the flower. Tie off the yarn ends. Crochet 10 flowers.

2   Trim away excess yarn from the back of each flower and add a dab of fabric glue. Glue the flowers in place on the front of the T-shirt and along the sleeve hemlines. Let dry.

Pocket Pattern, 100%

t·tip

Fun yarns in bright
colors offer a
lively look, while
soft pastel colors
will please every
sweet little girl's heart.

Popsicle Purple

materials list:

T-shirt, purple,
youth small (6/8)

¼ yd. (0.25 m)
patterned fabric, purple

⅛ yd. (0.15 m)
patterned fabric, green

paper

hand-sewing needle

two decorative buttons, ½" (1.3 cm)

Stitch up some fun in no time. Playing in the sand or walking along the boardwalk, your little one will be protected from the hot afternoon sun or a cool afternoon breeze in this playful cover-up.

Pattern, enlarge 200%

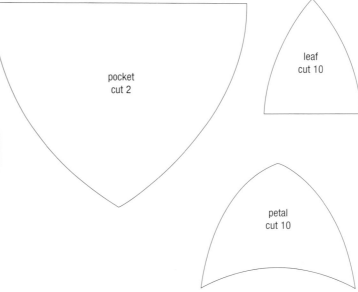

pocket
cut 2

leaf
cut 10

petal
cut 10

T-shirt Preparation

1   Measure, then cut, 3" (7.6 cm) up from the bottom hemline *through both layers* of the T-shirt.

2   Fold the shirt in half, matching the shoulder seams, and press a line down the center front of the T-shirt. Cut the front of the shirt open along the pressed line.

3   Stitch ⅛" (3 mm) from the hemline raw edges to stabilize the bottom of the shirt.

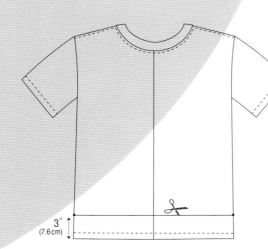

3"
(7.6 cm)

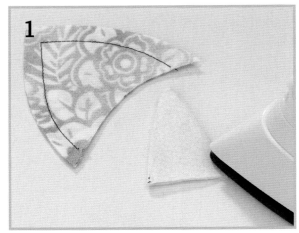

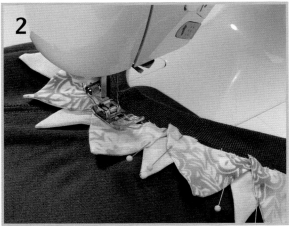

Construction Details, Ruffle

1 Measure the bottom of the T-shirt and multiply the distance by two. Cut a strip of purple fabric 3" (7.6 cm) wide by the total distance. Turn under the bottom edge of the strip ½" (1.3 cm) and press. Unfold and turn the raw edge in to meet the pressed fold; press again. Refold to form a double-folded hemline. Stitch close to the edge. Repeat the double hem on both 3" (7.6 cm) ends. Sew two rows of gathering stitches along the top edge, ⅛" (3 mm) and ¼" (6 mm) from the edge.

2 With right sides together, pin the end of the top edge of the ruffle strip to the bottom right front corner of the T-shirt. Pull the gathering threads and distribute gathers evenly along the length of the T-shirt, pinning as you go. Stitch a ¼" (6 mm) seam. Finish the raw edges of the ruffle and T-shirt with an overcast stitch. Press the ruffle down from the bottom of the T-shirt.

Construction Details, Neckline & Placket

1 Cut 14 petals from the purple fabric and 12 leaves from the green fabric. Match two petal sections, right sides together, and stitch a ⅜" (1 cm) seam, leaving the bottom edge open. Turn right side out and press. Repeat with the remaining petals and leaves.

2 Pin a petal 1" (2.5 cm) from the center front on the right side of the T-shirt, with the raw edge against the neckline ribbing seam line. Repeat on the left side. Tuck a second petal under the first petal, and continue placing and pinning on opposites sides around the neckline. Adjust the amount of petal overlap with the last petal to accommodate the T-shirt neckline. Center the leaves under the petals and pin. Baste the petals and leaves in place.

3 Roll the neckline ribbing to the right side of the T-shirt, covering the raw edges of the petals and the leaves; hand-stitch in place.

4 Measure the length of the front T-shirt opening. Cut two strips of patterned purple fabric 2" (5.1 cm) wide by the length plus 1" (2.5 cm) to create binding for the front opening. Turn the short ends over ½" (1.3 cm) and press.

5 Cut a 2" × 4" (5.1 × 10.2 cm) strip of the same fabric for the button loop.

6 Fold each of the three strips in half lengthwise, wrong sides together, and press. Open and fold the outside edges in to the fold line; press. Refold in half and press.

7 Open one length of binding and pin it, right sides together, to the right front edge of the T-shirt, matching the cut edges. Stitch the binding to the T-shirt in the fold. Wrap the binding to the back of the T-shirt and handstitch. Repeat the procedure on the left front.

8 Fold the 4" (10.2 cm) button loop strip in half again lengthwise and press. Topstitch through all the layers of fabric the length of the strip. Cross one end of the stitched strip over the other, forming a loop, and stitch to the neckline on the left side of the T-shirt. Stitch a decorative button on the opposite edge.

Designer Extra, Hair Tie

1   Cut a 1½" (3.8 cm) strip from the circumference of a purple T-shirt and another from a white T-shirt. Cut both strips in half vertically. Pull the strips taut to form a tube.

2   Place two white and one purple tube together then tack one end. Braid the three tubes; then sew the braided ends together.

3   Cut the fourth tube in half vertically. Wrap the tube over one end of the braid and stitch.
    Repeat on the other side.

Construction Details, Pockets

1   Trace the pocket pattern onto paper. Pin the pattern over two 5" (12.7 cm) squares of the purple fabric and cut, following the pattern lines. Cut a 1" × 5" (2.5 × 12.7 cm) strip of green fabric. Fold the strip in half lengthwise, wrong sides together, and press. Pin the edges of the strip to the top of one pocket section. Stitch a ¼" (6 mm) seam.

2   Press the strip up from the top of the pocket. Pin the pocket sections right sides together, and stitch along the edges, leaving a 2" (5.1 cm) opening. Turn right side out and press. Hand-stitch the opening closed. Topstitch the pocket in place to the left side of the T-shirt front.

3   Sew a button at the neckline and to the top of the pocket just below the green.

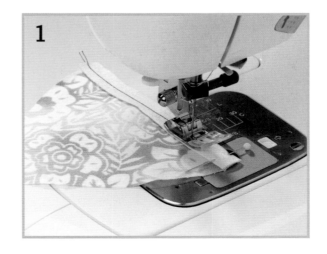

Crackerjack Green

materials list:

Coordinating fabrics make it easy to create this sweet version of a classic T-shirt spring dress.

T-shirt, white, toddler's,

¼ yd. (0.25 m) fabric, child's print

¼ yd. (0.25 m) fabric, coordinating child's print

four buttons

embroidery needle

embroidery thread

T-shirt Preparation

1   Measure, then cut, 5" (12.7 cm) up from the bottom hemline *through both layers* of the T-shirt.

2   Stitch ⅛" (3 mm) from the raw edges to stabilize the bottom.

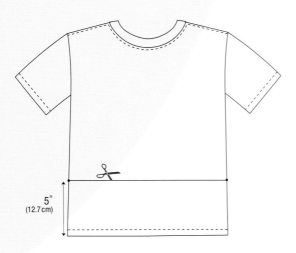

5"
(12.7 cm)

Construction Details

1 Cut a 6" (15.2 cm) strip the width of the fabric, from the main print for the skirt.

2 Fold the strip in half vertically, right sides together, and stitch forming a loop. Press. Sew two rows of gathering stitches along the top edge, ½" (1.3 cm) and ¼" (6 mm) from the edge.

3 Cut two 2" (5.1 cm) strips the width of the fabric from the coordinating print for the binding and the front placket.

4 To create the binding, fold one 2" (5.1 cm) strip in half lengthwise, wrong sides together, and press. Open, and then fold the outside edges to the center fold. Press. Refold in half and press. Encase the bottom edge of the skirt with the binding, overlap the opposite end, trim excess binding, and turn the end under. Topstitch through all layers of the fabric close to the folded edge of the binding.

5 Starting at the neckline, measure the length of the T-shirt at the center front and add ¾" (2 cm) to get the placket length. Trim a strip of 2" (5.1 cm) fabric to this length. Turn under both long edges of the placket piece ⅜" (1 cm) and press.

6 Carefully remove the stitching along the neckline binding at the center front of the T-shirt. Trim the top edge of the placket to match the curve of the neckline. Slide the placket under the neckline binding and pin in place. Pin the bottom edge of the placket to the bottom of the T-shirt. Topstitch through all layers, ¼" (6 mm) from the placket edge. To enclose the top edge of the placket and add a decorative touch, topstitch through all layers along the entire neckline binding, using a contrasting color thread.

7 Pin the skirt to the bottom of the T-shirt, right sides together. Pull the gathering threads and adjust the gathers evenly. Stitch the skirt to the T-shirt, right sides together, using a ½" (1.3 cm) seam. Finish the raw edges with an overcast stitch. Topstitch through all layers, ¼" (6 mm) from the waistline seam using a contrasting color thread.

8 Sew buttons to the front of the T-shirt, centering them on top of the front placket. Attach buttons by stitching from the front with the embroidery thread using the embroidery needle; finish by tying the thread ends together.

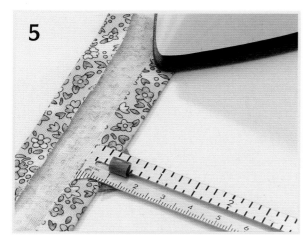

t·tip

Decorative buttons
are available in a variety
of themes. Choose your
supplies with fun in mind.
Attach buttons securely if the
garment is to be worn by a
young child as buttons pose a
potential choking danger.

Petal Perfect

The choice of soft colors, petals delicately placed around the neckline, and a flirty ruffle hemline are complemented with a fuzzy chenille rickrack trim.

materials list:

T-shirt, pink, toddler'

1/8" yd. (0.15 m) fabric

rickrack, chenille, medium

Pattern, enlarge 200%

Petal
cut 16

T-shirt Preparation

1   Remove the bottom hemline, cutting close to the stitching line.

Construction Details

1 Cut sixteen petals from the fabric using the pattern provided. Match two petal sections, right sides together, and stitch using a ¼" (6 mm) seam, leaving the bottom edge open. Turn right side out and press. Fold a small tuck in the center of each petal and pin. Repeat with the remaining petals.

2 Working with the first petal and starting at the center front on the right side of the T-shirt, place the raw edge of the petal against the neckline ribbing seam line. Stitch petals to the front of the T-shirt neckline using a zigzag stitch.

3 At the center back of the T-shirt, place a mark 4" (10.2 cm) down from the neckline and draw a line. Cut along the line. Turn the edges under ¹⁄₁₆" (1.6 mm) and topstitch.

4 Center the rickrack over the topstitching starting and ending just under the neckline ribbing along the back opening and pin. Stitch the rickrack over the topstitching. Trim the ends. Leaving 6" (15.2 cm) extending on both sides, pin rickrack along the edge of the neckline. Stitch in place starting from the back, continuing to the front, covering the raw edges of the petals, and ending at the back. Stitch the rickrack on top of the sleeve hemlines.

5 Measure the circumference of the bottom of the T-shirt and multiply this distance by two. Cut a strip of fabric 2" (5.1 cm) by this measurement. With right sides together, stitch the short ends of the strip together. Press the seam open. Turn under the bottom edge of the strip ½" (1.3 cm) and press. Unfold the edge and turn the raw edge in to meet the pressed fold; press again. Refold the edge, forming a double-folded hemline. Stitch along the edge of the inner fold. Sew two rows of gathering stitches along the top edge, ⅛" (3 mm) and ¼" (6 mm) from the edge.

6 With right sides together, pin the top edge of the ruffle strip to the bottom of the T-shirt. Pull the gathering threads and distribute the gathers evenly along the length of the ruffle. Stitch a ¼" (6 mm) seam. Finish the raw edges of the ruffle and T-shirt with an overcast stitch. Press the ruffle down from the bottom of the T-shirt.

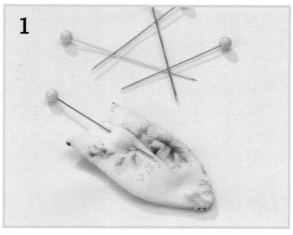

t·tip

Create a sweet ruffled brim hat or petal-trimmed purse to make this design doubly delightful.

Sources

STAMPS
Hot Potatoes Fabric & Rubber Stamps
Olive Dots #P421, Calypso Crochet
www.hotpotatoes.com

Plaid Enterprises, Inc.
Simply Stamps, Dandelion #54332, Tricolor Tropical
www.plaidonline.com

STENCILS
Plaid Enterprises, Inc.
Simply® Stencils #28499, Shades of Teal
Stencil Décor #26820, Spring Zinnias
www.plaidonline.com

PAINT
DecoArt™ Americana Acrylic Paint
Acrylic Paint & Fabric Painting Medium
Burnt Umber, Calypso Crochet
Snow White, Bubblegum Gingham
Snow White, Lemon Yellow, Sea Aqua, Electric Pink,
Tricolor Tropical
Snow White, Lavender, Spring Zinnia
Deep Teal, Shades of Teal
www.decoart.com

HOT-FIX CRYSTALS & NAILHEADS
3 mm Hot-Fix Swarovski® Xilion® Crystals & Purple
Crystals, Mulberry Beaded
Hot-Fix Nailheads, Caribbean Ribbons
3 mm Hot-Fix Swarovski® White Pearls, Black & White

APPLICATOR TOOL
Kandi Kane™, Mulberry Beaded, Caribbean Ribbons,
Black & White
www.KandiCorp.com

GLUE
Fabri-Tac™ Fabric Glue
Dazzle Tac Jewelry Glue™
Beacon™ Adhesives
www.beacon1.com

YARNS
Aunt Lydia's Beadies Crochet #0038 Surfer,
Flower Power
Coats & Clark
www.coatsandclark.com

MODA-DEA™
Fur Ever Yarn #3547 Limeade, Lime Sorbet
www.modadea.com

FUSIBLE WEB & TAPES
Steam-A-Seam2® Fusible Tapes
Steam-A Seam2® Double Stick Fusible Web
The Warm™ Company
www.warmcompany.com

SEWING MACHINE
Janome Memory Craft 6500P Sewing Machine
Janome America, Inc.
www.janome.com